Time to try.... the AUTOIMMUNE Diet

CookNation

Time to try... The Autoimmune Diet

Fix your diet, heal your gut & change your life

ISBN: 978-1-912511-53-2

DISCLAIMER

CONTENTS

Introduction 7

Autoimmune Breakfast

Coconut Flakes And Almond Milk 11
Watermelon, Mint And Avocado 12
Coconut And Banana Pancakes 13
Breakfast Hash 14
Breakfast Chicken Broth 15
Grapefruit and Oregano Grill 16
Cherry and Coconut Bowl 17
Pineapple and Tarragon Oil 18
Turkey and Sweet Apple Morning Kebabs 19
Cucumber Wedges with Avocado Cream 20
Breakfast Salad 21
Autoimmune Porridge Pot 22
Smoothie Bowl 23
Tropical Smoothie Bowl 24
Stewed Apples and Coconut Crumb 25
Banana and Blueberry Muffins 26
27

Autoimmune Lunch

Crispy Salmon Broth 29
Calamari and Cucumber Salad 30
Peach and Chicken Salad 31
Cauliflower and Leek Soup 32
Warm Roasted Vegetable Salad 33
Broccoli & Watercress Soup with Basil Oil 34
Mushroom, Sage and Bacon Roll Ups 35
36

Savoury Cassava Biscuits with Sardines 37
Stir Fry Salad 38
Grilled Asparagus with Lemon Cream 39
Summer Herb Bowl and Mustard Drizzle 40
Strawberry Fields 41
Sunday Veg Bowl 42
Spiced Chicken Flatbread 43
Spiced Raw Cauliflower 44
Tuna and Red Onion Packed Lunch 45

Autoimmune Dinner 47
Pork Grilled & Pineapple and Bowl 48
Tuna and Caramelised Onion Pizza 49
Pork, Sweet Potato and Apple Bake 50
Pork Chops with Mango Relish 51
Meatballs and Courgetti 52
Prawn and Asparagus "Risotto" 53
Baked Potatoes with Chicken Liver 54
Cod Laksa 55
Roast Chicken with Salsa Verde 56
Spring Vegetables and Herb Chicken 57
Braised Turkey With Gremolata 58
Venison and Cranberry Hot Pot 59
Grilled Mackerel,Apples & Sauerkraut 60
Liver, Onion and "Mash" 61
Garlic and Lemon Kebabs 62
Lamb and Cauliflower 'Rice' 63

Autoimmune Dessert 65
Baked Apples with Cinnamon Crunch 66
Banana Bread Pudding With Cacao Nibs 67
Mango Ice with Mint Crunch 68
Pear Crunch 69
Banana and Berry Ice 70

Raspberry Shortcake 71
Autoimmune Brownie 72
Blueberry Cobbler 73
Gooseberry And Ginger Galette 74
Grilled Bananas With Passionfruit Drizzle 75
Blackberries And Cream Parfait 76
Mint Choc Ice 77
Ginger And Apricot Pudding 78
Apple And Cinnamon Pudding 79
Fruit Kebab With Lemon And Basil Dressing 80
Pumpkin Panna Cotta With Stewed Pears 81

Autoimmune Snacks 83
Kiwi And Banana Power Smoothie 84
Elderflower And Ginger Smoothie 85
Cucumber, Spinach And Apple Quencher 86
Passionfruit And Melon Energy Drink 87
Cinnamon Hot Chocolate 88
Coconut Fat Bomb Smoothie 89
Indulgent Spiced Brownie Smoothie 90
Blueberry, Lime And Mint Tonic 91
Ginger And Coconut Bounce Balls 92
Gummy Sweets 93
Kale Crisps 94
Honey Cookies 95
Courgette/Zucchini Chips 96

INTRODUCTION

Your diet plays a huge part in reversing, treating and controlling chronic, inflammatory illness and the Autoimmune Diet approach is a fantastic tool for making sense of what you eat, to keep you being the best you can.

Many of us suffer with physical symptoms on a daily basis that we associate with "tiredness" and "stress" and happily go about taking over-the-counter remedies or suffer in silence to deal with them.

Inflammatory processes can start for many months or even years before a firm diagnosis or condition is confirmed and whilst we ignore many of the first signs, there are many things you can do from the start to help slow disease progression and maybe prevent it in the first place.

Your diet plays a huge part of reversing, treating and controlling chronic, inflammatory illness and the Autoimmune Diet is a fantastic tool for making sense of what you eat, to keep you being the best you can.

The Autoimmune Diet considers the inflammation in our bodies is caused by a leak of some of the diverse, well developed bacteria we have in our stomachs. This inflammation can start off hardly noticeable as you go about your daily life, but it is possible to be aware of these symptoms early on and to take action.

By managing the types of food you eat, you can improve, prevent and reverse debilitating conditions now and in the future. Working towards building a stronger intestinal lining and removing foods from your diet, known to cause inflammation, is what the Autoimmune Diet teaches and so many have found this natural lifestyle and diet to be extremely successful.

When the body begins to react to a leaky gut, it starts to attack. However, instead of just targeting foreign invaders, it starts to attack healthy tissue too. This can begin in the thyroid gland, salivary gland and brain tissue to name a few places. Although no one knows exactly what triggers autoimmune disease, it is thought there is an association with different types of bacteria. Conditions, such as multiple sclerosis, asthma, arthritis, allergies, lupus, chronic fatigue syndrome, rheumatic fever and ankylosing spondylitis are just a few of these autoimmune diseases.

Some of the mild symptoms of a leaky gut can be: ulcers, headaches, irregular heartbeat, nasal congestion, poor eye sight, poor memory and brain fog, shortness of breath, earaches, trouble sleeping, fatigue, bloating, indigestion, diarrhoea, weight gain, joint pain and stiffness, anxiety, depression and irritability. All quite vague symptoms really, that many experience just due to lifestyle.

If you are someone that suffers with a number of these mild symptoms, the Autoimmune Diet may be of great help to you and possibly prevent future symptoms worsening and becoming really troublesome. Investigating this approach to your lifestyle and diet will be paramount to its success in the long run and there are well trained Autoimmune Diet coaches out there who can really get you started on a positive step. However, you can implement these changes with a bit of common sense, well researched knowledge and determination yourself.

The approach on an Autoimmune Diet eating plan is to:

1. Remove the foods from your diet that are toxic or inflammatory.
2. Build and restore the bacteria in your gut to be healthy, diverse and balanced.
3. Repair the gut. Gelatine, collagen and other supplements and nutrients can help to do this.

Ingredients

There is no denying that only eating foods on the Autoimmune Diet is a difficult thing to do in the beginning. You will be re-educating yourself with shopping, cooking and preparing and there will be many ingredients you may find yourself missing. However, it is important to see these changes as a minor inconvenience at the beginning of a long-term investment in your health and it ***IS*** possible to enjoy these foods and embrace these changes.

Removing grains, gluten and legumes is a large group of foods that provide the base and energy for many of our diets, so this needs to be re-established. Reaching for different flour types, energy foods and snacks will be necessary and if you have an unknown sensitivity to any of these ingredients, you may find an instant improvement in your physical self.

Nuts, seeds, lentils, beans and grains are all removed from the diet and these are sometimes the hardest changes to establish. Many of us who follow reasonably healthy diets already, include these types of food in our store cupboards and it can take some effort to eliminate them!

Also removing ingredients that are deemed toxic, such as processed foods, trans fats and sugars can also prove troublesome. Many snacks and drinks we reach for in hunger contain these toxic elements, so introducing homemade snacks and a cupboard and fridge full of friendly foods is key.

So, to look at the core ingredients of the Autoimmune Diet, these have been broken down into categories to make it simple and easy to follow. As you become more confident in your choices, you can research more and be increasingly adventurous in your food preparation.

Flours

Arrowroot starch/flour, cassava flour, coconut flour and tigernut flour can all be used on an Autoimmune Diet and although they behave quite differently to gluten flours, baking can be adapted and recipes changed to produce some great results.
Baking powder can be used to help bakes to raise but make you choose a gluten free variety.

Fats

The right fats in your diet only help your health, not hinder it. They can provide support for healthy cell membranes, the nervous system and also enable the body to absorb the fat-soluble vitamins, such as A, D, K and E. They

shouldn't be avoided - the right fats should be chosen, and they should always be organic, where possible.
Avocado oil, coconut oil, olive oil, toasted sesame oil flaxseed oil, lard/dripping, palm oil and grapeseed oil are all allowed on an Autoimmune diet and they all have different uses.
Cooking should be done with olive oil, coconut oil, avocado oil and lard/dripping. Dressings can use the fats that have lower smoking points, such as toasted sesame oil and flaxseed oil.
Baking can be used by a mix of these fats.

Vegetables and Fruit

Almost all can be eaten in abundance (although fruit in moderation) so it is easier to list the ones you CAN'T eat:
All nightshade plants – such as aubergines, tomatoes, peppers, goji berries and potatoes. Avoid green beans, sugar snap peas, peas and edamame beans.
These vegetables are all considered inflammatory.

Coconut

Coconut products are a saviour. They provide dense nutrition and versatile ingredients and can be used in a variety of ways.
Coconut oil, coconut butter, coconut sugar, coconut aminos, coconut cream, coconut milk, coconut flour and coconut flakes are all available as part of an Autoimmune Diet eating plan and they can create a wealth of textures, flavour and combinations.

Condiments, Spices and Flavours

You may wish to add some full-on flavour to your cooking and this is possible. However, some of the "usuals" are not permitted, such as peppers, chillis and tomatoes so some creative thinking is needed. The following are all allowed to be added:
Fish sauce, salt (not pepper), mustard (check ingredients), ginger (fresh root and dried), garlic, fresh herbs, turmeric, vinegar (check yeast hasn't been added), coconut aminos (instead of soy sauce), stock and bone broth.

Snacks

Dried seaweed, dehydrated vegetables and fruits, meat jerky, fresh fruit, roasted vegetables, tigernuts, flaked coconut, to name a few. We have included some delicious (and sometimes indulgent) ideas and recipes in this cookbook.

Sweeteners

Sugar is added to so many processed foods and if you were to count up the amount of sugar you consume in a day you would be shocked. This can be through jar sauces, coffees, other drinks, cereals, crisps, dressings and general baked goods. It all adds up!
Sugar is a toxic element to our diets and the Autoimmune approach will encourage you to bake and make your dishes from scratch,
Sweeteners are allowed, but you must ensure you use these sparingly. They are:
Raw honey (do not give this to under 1's), maple syrup, coconut sugar, molasses (the blackstrap variety has much more nutritional value) and stevia.

Proteins

All grass fed and organic wherever possible. Farmers are known to give their livestock unnecessary drugs and medications and the only way to avoid traces of these in your meat, is to avoid mass produced, cheap protein.
Beef, turkey, pork (ham and bacon too), lamb, offal, chicken, game, fish and shellfish can all be enjoyed on an Autoimmune Diet plan.
Avoid eggs and dairy though, these are considered to cause inflammation. Animal milk, cream and cheese are all off limits.

Fermented Foods

Avoid fermented soy, but you can enjoy kefir, sauerkraut and kimchi freely. No Soy. Tofu is not permitted and is considered an inflammatory food.

Collagen and Gelatine

These are commonly added due to their nutritional value and ability to help restore and repair the gut lining. They can thicken up dishes and add binding agents where eggs would have been, and they create some great smoothies.
Gelatine creates a gel like texture that is essential for baking.
Collagen is tasteless and can easily be added to drinks and is available in supermarkets.
Both gelatine and collagen are great sources of many amino acids that are essential to your wellbeing and a great aid.
When purchasing these products ensure they are natural, Autoimmune Diet-friendly, with no added gluten.

An Autoimmune Diet approach to your eating is embracing a new lifestyle. You can take control of unnecessary symptoms, feel energized, healthy and happy. There is a wealth of information on the internet to study if you wish and you can become an oracle of knowledge on the subject. **Time to try... The Autoimmune Diet** aims to gradually introduce beginners to the process and lifestyle and inspire a new way of eating.

Take notice of your body, the foods you eat and give your body the respect it deserves. Exercise a little more and take time to consider the fuel you are giving it. To eliminate inflammation from your body and the damage it is doing, embrace the Autoimmune solution and all the good health it can bring.

About CookNation

CookNation is the leading publisher of innovative and practical recipe books for the modern, health conscious cook. CookNation titles bring together delicious, easy and practical recipes with their unique no-nonsense approach - making cooking for diets and healthy eating fast, simple and fun.

With a range of #1 best-selling titles - from the innovative 'Skinny' calorie-counted series, to the 5:2 Diet Recipes collection - CookNation recipe books prove that 'Diet' can still mean 'Delicious'!

CookNation

Time to try....

AUTOIMMUNE

BREAKFAST

SERVES 3

COCONUT FLAKES AND ALMOND MILK

Time to try....
AI diet

Ingredients

- 2 tbsp coconut oil
- 1 tsp vanilla extract
- 225g/8oz coconut flakes
- 500ml/2 cups unsweetened almond milk to serve

Method

1 Heat the oil in a frying pan. Add the vanilla extract and stir well.

2 Tip the coconut flakes into the oil and stir for 4-5 minutes.

3 When evenly toasted, remove from the pan and drain on kitchen towel.

4 Allow to cool completely then serve with almond milk.

5 Any unused flakes can be stored in an air tight container.

CHEF'S NOTE

You could serve this flaked breakfast with fresh blueberries, raspberries or strawberries.

SERVES 1

WATERMELON, MINT AND AVOCADO

Time to try....
AI diet

Ingredients

- ½ an avocado
- 4 slices of watermelon
- 1 tbsp chopped fresh mint leaves
- 2 tbsp lemon juice
- 1 tsp balsamic vinegar

Method

1 Remove the peel and de-stone the avocado. Slice thinly.

2 Remove the skin from the watermelon and slice.

3 Alternate strips of avocado and watermelon across a plate.

4 Sprinkle over the chopped mint.

5 Mix the lemon juice, zest and balsamic vinegar together and drizzle over the top.

6 Serve immediately.

CHEF'S NOTE

No waste: If you leave the stone in the other half of the avocado and wrap tightly in cling film, you should find it won't discolour and it can be used the next day.

SERVES 1

COCONUT AND BANANA PANCAKES

Time to try.... AI diet

Ingredients

- 1 small banana
- 1 tbsp coconut flour
- 1 tbsp desiccated coconut
- ½ tsp ground cinnamon
- 1 tsp coconut oil
- 2 tbsp raspberries
- 1-2 tsp maple syrup

Method

1 Mash the banana with the back of a fork until smooth.

2 Stir in the coconut flour, desiccated coconut and cinnamon to form a thick dough.

3 Heat the oil in a frying pan.

4 Add the dough in heaped tablespoons to the oil and cook on both sides for 1-2 minutes.

5 Serve immediately with the raspberries and the maple syrup drizzled over.

CHEF'S NOTE

Maple syrup is one of sweeteners available to use (in moderation), but you could use honey, stevia, molasses or coconut sugar too.

BREAKFAST HASH

SERVES 2

Time to try.... AI diet

Ingredients

- 1 tbsp olive oil
- 175g/6oz bacon, chopped
- 1 onion, diced
- 1 small sweet potato, cut in to small dice
- 1 red apple, cored and cut into wedges
- 1 tbsp lemon juice
- 1 tsp chopped fresh sage
- 1 tsp pink Himalayan sea salt

Method

1 Heat the olive oil in a large frying pan. Add the bacon and fry over a high heat until browned.

2 Add the onion and the sweet potato and stir to coat in the bacon and oil. Add a splash of water if it is a little dry.

3 Stir over a medium heat for 10-15 minutes until the potato is just about cooked through and soft.

4 Add the apple wedges and lemon juice and continue to cook until the apple and the potatoes are a little crisp.

5 Add the chopped sage and salt to the pan and stir for a further 1 minute before serving between 2 plates.

CHEF'S NOTE

Use a good quality bacon here to make the most of the Autoimmune Diet friendly protein in this dish.

SERVES 1

BREAKFAST CHICKEN BROTH

Time to try.... AI diet

Ingredients

- 300ml/10½floz bone broth
- 3 spring onions, sliced
- 1 handful of shredded cooked chicken
- 1 tbsp flat leaf parsley, chopped
- 4 red radishes, thinly sliced
- Pinch of pink Himalayan Sea Salt

Method

1 Heat the bone broth in a small saucepan.

2 Add the spring onion and shredded chicken. Stir until well mixed and heated through.

3 Add the parsley and radishes and heat through.

4 Add the salt and pour in to a serving bowl.

CHEF'S NOTE

Bone broth contains healing compounds, such as collagen, which is thought to help restore gut lining.

SERVES 1

GRAPEFRUIT AND OREGANO GRILL

Time to try....
AI
diet

Ingredients

- 1 large pink grapefruit
- 1 tsp coconut sugar
- 1 tbsp fresh oregano, chopped
- ½ tsp fresh thyme leaves

Method

1 Preheat the grill.

2 Halve the grapefruit and place on a baking tray that will fit under your grill.

3 Mix the coconut sugar and herbs together and sprinkle over the two halves of grapefuit.

4 Grill for 4-5 minutes until the top is a little crisp, but don't allow the herbs to burn.

5 Serve immediately.

CHEF'S NOTE

Grapefruit is a great breakfast fruit if you are trying to remain focused on your eating plan. It can act as a hunger suppressant and may reduce the mid-morning snack attack!

SERVES 1

CHERRY AND COCONUT BOWL

Time to try....
AI diet

Ingredients

- 150g/5oz fresh organic cherries, stones removed
- 1 tbsp water
- 1 tbsp coconut flakes
- 100g/3½oz coconut milk yoghurt

Method

1 Make sure all of the stones are removed from the cherries.

2 Add to the bowl of a high-speed blender (reserve a couple for decoration) with the water and process until smooth.

3 Toast the coconut flakes in a non-stick pan. Cool a little.

4 Add the coconut yoghurt into a small bowl.

5 Carefully, run a line of cherry puree across the top of the yoghurt.

6 Chop the reserved cherries. Add the coconut flakes and chopped cherries to the top.

CHEF'S NOTE

Use organic cherries as they have more anti-oxidants benefits.

SERVES 1

PINEAPPLE AND TARRAGON OIL

Time to try....
AI diet

Ingredients

- 3 large slices of pineapple
- 1 tbsp olive oil
- 1 tbsp fresh tarragon leaves, chopped

Method

1 Mix the oil and tarragon leaves together and leave at room temperature for an hour if possible.

2 Place the pineapple onto a plate, fanning out the pieces

3 Pour on the tarragon oil and serve immediately.

CHEF'S NOTE

Pineapple contains the enzyme bromelain, which can help reduce inflammation.

SERVES 2

TURKEY AND SWEET APPLE MORNING KEBABS

Time to try... AI diet

Ingredients

- 400g/14oz turkey mince
- 1 dessert apple, cored and grated
- 1 tsp fresh sage, chopped
- ¼ tsp ground nutmeg
- ½ tsp pink Himalayan sea salt
- 1 tsp olive oil
- ½ romaine lettuce, shredded
- 1 celery stalk, finely sliced

Method

1. Preheat the grill while you mix the turkey mince, apple, sage, nutmeg and salt together.
2. Shape into 6 "sausage shapes" and thread onto 6 metal skewers.
3. Rub the olive oil over a baking sheet that will fit under your grill and place the skewers on top.
4. Place the baking tray under a hot grill and cook for 12-15 minutes, turning half way through.
5. When coloured and cooked through, remove to cool a little.
6. Divide the lettuce and celery between 2 plates.
7. Top the lettuce with 3 kebabs on each plate.

CHEF'S NOTE

Embrace some savoury flavours for breakfast as part of your diet. You won't miss sugary cereals in the end and your body will thank you for it.

SERVES 1

CUCUMBER WEDGES WITH AVOCADO CREAM

Time to try....
AI
diet

Ingredients

- Handful of baby spinach leaves
- ½ medium cucumber
- ½ avocado
- 1 tbsp coconut yoghurt
- Pinch of pink Himalayan sea salt
- 1 tbsp fresh dill fronds

Method

1 Spread the spinach leaves on a plate.

2 Cut the cucumber lengthways into thick slices and fan out on top of the leaves.

3 Remove the peel and stone from the avocado and mash together with the yoghurt and salt, until smooth and creamy.

4 Mix the dill into the avocado cream, leaving a little to one side.

5 Spoon the cream on top of the cucumber and scatter over the reserved dill fronds.

CHEF'S NOTE

Cucumbers should be eaten with the skin on, to ensure you get the full benefits of the anti-inflammatory properties they contain.

BREAKFAST SALAD

SERVES 2

Time to try...
AI diet

Ingredients

- 1 banana
- ½ iceberg lettuce
- 1 apple, cored and thinly sliced
- 5-6 grapes
- ½ red grapefruit
- 2 tbsp coconut shreds
- 1 tbsp lemon juice
- 1 tbsp lemon zest
- 1 tbsp avocado oil

Method

1 Peel and slice the banana and shred the iceberg lettuce.

2 Halve the grapes and remove the pith and peel from the grapefruit.

3 Mix the avocado oil with the lemon juice and lemon zest.

4 In a large bowl, mix the banana, lettuce, grapes and grapefruit together.

5 Divide the salad between 2 plates and drizzle with the avocado oil and lemon dressing.

CHEF'S NOTE

Grapefruit is a great source of both vitamin A and C, vital for support your immune system.

SERVES 1

AUTOIMMUNE PORRIDGE POT

Time to try... AI diet

Ingredients

- 2 tbsp desiccated coconut
- 1 tbsp coconut flour
- 240ml/8floz coconut milk
- 1 tsp ground cinnamon
- 2 tsp collagen powder
- 1 banana

Method

1 Place the desiccated coconut, coconut flour, coconut milk, cinnamon and collagen powder in a small saucepan and gently heat.

2 Simmer for 10-15 minutes until thickened.

3 Peel and mash the banana until quite smooth.

4 Stir the banana into the milk mix and heat through.

5 Serve with an extra sprinkle of cinnamon.

CHEF'S NOTE

Collagen powder is a great asset to an Autoimmune Diet eating plan –it can help heal the lining of the intestinal wall and assist with the issues of a leaky gut.

SERVES 1

SMOOTHIE BOWL

Time to try....
AI diet

Ingredients

- 1 tsp coconut flakes
- 1 tbsp tigernuts, sliced
- 1 tbsp olive oil
- 1 banana
- 150g/5oz blueberries
- 125g/4oz raspberries
- 100ml/3½floz coconut milk
- Extra raspberries and blueberries for decoration

Method

1 Heat the oil in a small pan and add the tigernuts & coconut flakes. Stir for 2-3 minutes until toasted. Leave to cool.

2 Add the banana, blueberries, raspberries and coconut milk to a blender and process until really smooth.

3 Pour the smoothie mix into a bowl.

4 Top with the coconut flakes and tigernuts and extra fruit, to decorate.

5 Enjoy immediately.

CHEF'S NOTE

Make the most of the seasonal fruit available to you to get the best nutrition possible and always try to use organic.

SERVES 1

TROPICAL SMOOTHIE BOWL

Time to try...
AI diet

Ingredients

- 1 banana
- 150g/5oz any melon
- 125g/4oz fresh pineapple
- 1 tbsp coconut cream
- 1 passion fruit
- 2 tbsp coconut flakes

Method

1 Add the banana, melon, pineapple and coconut cream to a blender and process until smooth.

2 Halve the passion fruit and remove half of the seeds, reserve the other half.

3 Stir the passion fruit seeds through the smoothie and pour into a bowl.

4 Add the coconut flakes to the top and add the reserved passion fruit seeds.

5 Enjoy immediately.

CHEF'S NOTE

Smoothie bowls are so adaptable for those following special diets. You can create some fantastic colours and textures to celebrate all the foods you can eat. Mix them up to get the most diverse vitamins and minerals.

SERVES 1

STEWED APPLES AND COCONUT CRUMB

Time to try....
AI diet

Ingredients

- 1 tbsp coconut oil
- 1 tbsp coconut flour
- 1 tbsp desiccated coconut
- ½ tsp honey
- 2 large apples
- 1 tsp ground cinnamon
- ½ tsp ground ginger
- 1 tbsp coconut yoghurt

Method

1 Heat the coconut oil in a saucepan and add the flour and desiccated coconut and honey. Stir for 2-3 minutes until everything is quite toasted, sweet and clumping together. Leave to cool.

2 Core, peel the apples and slice them and add them to a saucepan with a splash of water.

3 Cook over a gentle heat until the apples are softened and breaking down.

4 Stir in the spices. Remove from the heat and leave to cool in the fridge.

5 When ready to serve, pour into a bowl and top with the coconut yoghurt and coconut crumb.

CHEF'S NOTE

Apples are a great source of fibre and can assist with stomach issues.

MAKES 8

BANANA AND BLUEBERRY MUFFINS

Time to try... AI diet

Ingredients

- 125g/4oz cassava flour
- 2 tbsp coconut flour
- ¼ cup coconut sugar
- 1 tsp ground cinnamon
- 1 tsp baking powder (gluten free)
- 2 bananas, very ripe
- ¼ cup of coconut oil
- 100g/3½oz blueberries
- 1 gelatin egg (1 tbsp gelatine + 4 tbsp water)

Method

1 In a bowl, mix the flours, sugar, cinnamon and baking powder together.

2 Mash the bananas together until really smooth.

3 To make the gelatine egg, slowly pour the 4 tbsp of water over the gelatine in a small saucepan and keep off the heat, to allow to harden a little for 2-3 minutes. Add the saucepan to the heat and then whisk hard for 1-2 minutes until the mixture becomes quite frothy. Add this "egg" to the dry mix.

4 Stir the bananas into the mix and beat until smooth.

5 Stir in the blueberries.

6 Preheat the oven to 375°F/190°C/Gas Mark 5 and line a muffin hole tin with 8 cases. Divide the mixture between the cases.

7 Bake for 15-20 minutes or until golden and a little risen. Remove from the oven and enjoy whilst still warm.

CHEF'S NOTE

"Gelatine eggs" are a good ingredient for binding in Autoimmune Diet baking recipes as they behave in a similar way to real eggs.

Time to try....

AUTOIMMUNE

LUNCH

SERVES 2

CRISPY SALMON BROTH

Time to try...
AI diet

Ingredients

- 1 tbsp coconut oil
- 2 small salmon fillets, skin on
- 450ml/15½floz chicken bone broth/stock
- 2 tsp fish sauce
- 1 tbsp lime juice
- 2 tbsp coconut aminos
- 1 tbsp grated fresh ginger root
- 1 garlic clove, crushed
- 3 spring onions, shredded
- 2 heads of pak choi, sliced in half lengthways
- 4 radishes shredded
- 1 tbsp fresh coriander/cilantro, chopped

Method

1 Heat the oil in a frying pan.

2 Add the salmon, skin side down and cook over a high heat for approximately 8 minutes. You want the skin really crisp. Repeat on the other side for 3-4 minutes, until just cooked through.

3 Meanwhile, heat the bone broth or stock in a saucepan.

4 Stir in the fish sauce, lime juice and coconut aminos and bring to a simmer.

5 Grate in the ginger and add the garlic and spring onions.

6 Next, add the pak choi and simmer for 3-4 minutes until softened.

7 Place a salmon fillet, skin side up in a bowl. Pour the broth and half of the vegetables around the fish.

8 Scatter over the radish and coriander/cilantro and serve immediately.

CHEF'S NOTE

Use coconut aminos in place of soy sauce. Made from coconut sap, it's sweet and salty and a good substitute.

SERVES 2

CALAMARI AND CUCUMBER SALAD

Time to try... AI diet

Ingredients

- 2 tbsp coconut flour
- 1 tsp pink Himalayan sea salt
- 1 tbsp fresh parsley, chopped
- 400g/14oz squid rings
- 1 lemon, cut into wedges
- 2 tbsp lemon juice
- 1 tbsp avocado oil
- 1 large cucumber
- Extra olive oil for frying

Method

1 Place the coconut flour, salt and fresh parsley into a freezer/food bag. Add the squid rings and give a good shake.

2 Heat a large frying pan and add 1-2cm of olive oil to the bottom. When really hot, dust the excess flour off the squid and cook in the oil, in batches.

3 Cook for 2-3 minutes on both sides and then drain on a kitchen towel.

4 Meanwhile, cut the cucumber into batons and place on two plates.

5 Mix the avocado oil with the lemon juice and drizzle over the cucumber.

6 Divide the squid between the two plates and serve with wedges of lemon.

CHEF'S NOTE

Squid is known to help the body reduce inflammation and it's also serves up a great hit of protein.

SERVES 1

PEACH AND CHICKEN SALAD

Time to try....
AI diet

Ingredients

- 1 ripe peach
- 1 cooked chicken breast, shredded
- 3 salad onions, chopped
- 1 tbsp fresh oregano leaves, chopped
- 50g/2oz rocket leaves
- 1 celery stalk, sliced thinly
- 1 tsp white wine vinegar
- 1 tbsp olive oil
- 1 tbsp lemon juice
- Pinch of Himalayan sea salt

Method

1. Halve the peach and remove the stone. Slice thinly.
2. Add the peach slices to a bowl and mix with the chicken, salad onions, oregano leaves, rocket and celery slices.
3. Mix the white wine vinegar, olive oil, salt and lemon juice together to make a dressing.
4. Tip the mixed salad onto a plate or into a bowl and drizzle over the dressing.
5. Serve immediately.

CHEF'S NOTE

Peaches are a great source of caffeic acid, which is a powerful anti-oxidant.

SERVES 2

CAULIFLOWER AND LEEK SOUP

Time to try... AI diet

Ingredients

- 1 small head of cauliflower
- 1 tbsp olive oil
- 1 onion, diced
- 1 leek, diced
- ½ fennel bulb, sliced and chopped finely
- 600ml/1 pint bone broth or chicken stock
- 1 tbsp lemon juice
- 1 tbsp fresh thyme, chopped
- ½ tsp pink Himalayan sea salt

Method

1 Remove the leaves from the cauliflower and cut the florets into small pieces.

2 Heat the olive oil in a saucepan. Add the onion and stir to coat. Cook over a medium heat for 4-5 minutes, to soften.

3 Add the leek and diced fennel and carry on cooking to soften the vegetables.

4 Add the cauliflower, bone broth/stock, lemon, thyme and salt and stir.

5 Bring to a simmer, add a lid to the saucepan and cook for 9-10 minutes over a low heat until the cauliflower has softened.

6 Using a stick blender, partially blend the soup so there are still chunks of vegetables in it.

CHEF'S NOTE

One serving of cauliflower gives you ¾ of your recommended Vitamin C intake, which is crucial for a healthy immune system.

SERVES 2

WARM ROASTED VEGETABLE SALAD

Time to try....
AI
diet

Ingredients

- 2 tbsp olive oil
- 1 red onion
- 8 chestnut mushrooms
- ½ fennel bulb
- 2 cloves of garlic
- 4 parsnips, peeled
- 150g/5oz baby spinach leaves
- 1 tsp apple cider vinegar
- Pinch of pink Himalayan Sea Salt
- 1 tbsp olive oil
- 1 tbsp lemon juice

Method

1 Pre-heat the oven to 375°F/190°C/Gas Mark 5

2 Cut the red onion into wedges

3 Halve or quarter the mushrooms (depending on how large they are).

4 Slice the fennel bulb and crush the garlic cloves.

5 Cut the parsnips length ways to make long strips.

6 Mix all of the ingredients together and tip onto a greased baking tray.

7 Tip over the olive oil and massage into all of the ingredients.

8 Place in the oven and roast for 20-25 minutes until everything is cooked and a little charred.

9 Mix the vinegar, salt, extra oil and lemon juice together.

10 Divide the spinach leaves between two plates and divide the vegetables between them too, placing them warm, on top.

11 Drizzle over the dressing and serve immediately.

CHEF'S NOTE

Roasting vegetables as part of an Autoimmune Diet diet is a great idea as it can add different textures and a lovely sweetness that is totally natural.

SERVES 2

BROCCOLI & WATERCRESS SOUP WITH BASIL OIL

Time to try... AI diet

Ingredients

- 2 tbsp olive oil
- 2 tbsp chopped fresh basil leaves
- ¼ pink Himalayan sea salt
- 1 tsp Olive Oil
- 200g/7oz watercress, large stalks removed
- 1 small head of broccoli, cut in to small florets
- 1 onion, diced
- 600ml/1 pint bone broth/chicken/vegetable stock
- 1 tbsp collagen powder

Method

1 Mix the olive oil with the basil leaves and salt. Leave to infuse and for the flavours to develop for up to 24 hours.

2 Heat the oil for the soup in a saucepan and add the onion. Stir over a medium heat for 4-5 minutes to soften.

3 Add the broccoli, watercress, bone broth/stock and collagen and bring to a simmer.

4 Cook for 9-10 minutes or until the broccoli is soft.

5 Using a stick blender or soup blender, process the soup until really smooth.

6 Divide between 2 bowls and drizzle over the basil oil.

CHEF'S NOTE

Basil is a known anti-oxidant and contains enzyme inhibiting oils, which help reduce inflammation in the body.

SERVES 1

MUSHROOM, SAGE AND BACON ROLL UPS

Time to try... AI diet

Ingredients

- 6 chestnut mushrooms
- 6 thin slices of streaky bacon
- 6 small sage leaves
- 1 apple, sliced
- 1 small handful of watercress leaves (thick stalks removed)

Method

1. Pre-heat the oven to 400˚F/200˚C/Gas Mark 6 and grease a baking tray.
2. On a board, place all 6 mushrooms.
3. Lay the bacon strips flat down and place sage leaf on each.
4. Place a mushroom on each bacon strip and roll up very tightly.
5. Place all 6 roll ups on the baking tray and bake in the oven for 15-20 minutes until cooked and crisp.
6. Place the watercress and apple on a plate and put the roll ups on top.

CHEF'S NOTE

Sage is known to help with digestive issues, such as cramps and indigestion and acts as a soothing aid to stomach complaints.

SERVES 2

SAVOURY CASSAVA BISCUITS WITH SARDINES

Time to try.... AI diet

Ingredients

- 175g/6oz cassava flour
- 2 tsp baking powder (gluten free)
- ¼ tsp pink Himalayan sea salt
- 2 tbsp coconut oil, melted
- 200ml/7floz coconut milk
- 1 tbsp lemon juice
- 1 tbsp fresh oregano leaves, chopped
- 2x 90g tins of sardines in olive oil
- 1 handful of rocket leaves
- Wedges of lemon

Method

1 Pre-heat the oven to 400°F/200°C/Gas Mark 6.

2 To make the biscuits, mix the flour, baking powder, salt, coconut oil, coconut milk and oregano together. Adjust the quantity of milk, if need be, to create a firm dough.

3 Roll out the dough to about 2cm deep and cut 9 cookie shapes out.

4 Place on a greased baking tray and bake in the oven for 15-20 minutes, or until risen and cooked.

5 Slice 2 of the biscuits in half (keep the others stored for another time) and place cut side up, on a tray that will go under the grill.

6 Mash the sardines from the tin and spread on top of the biscuits.

7 Place the tray under a hot grill and toast until the sardines are crisped and heated through.

8 Put 2 halves on one plate each and top with some rocket leaves and a lemon wedge.

CHEF'S NOTE

Tinned sardines are a store cupboard essential. Full of omega-3 and calcium, but make sure you only get the ones packed in olive oil and not tomato sauce!

SERVES 1

STIR FRY SALAD

Time to try.... AI diet

Ingredients

- 1 tbsp olive oil
- 6 Brussels sprouts, shredded
- 2 leaves of Chinese lettuce, shredded
- 3 chestnut mushrooms, sliced
- 1 red onion, halved and sliced
- 1 garlic clove, crushed
- 1 tsp fresh grated ginger root

For The Dressing

- ½ tbsp coconut aminos
- 1 tbsp lime juice
- 1 tbsp olive oil
- ½ tsp pink Himalayan sea salt

Method

1 Heat the olive oil in a large frying pan or wok.

2 Add the Brussels sprouts, Chinese lettuce, mushrooms, red onion, garlic and ginger.

3 Stir fry for 9-10 minutes until the vegetables are soft but still with a little crunch.

4 Place everything into a bowl or on a plate.

5 Mix together all of the dressing ingredients and drizzle over the salad.

CHEF'S NOTE

Brussels sprouts are part of the cruciferous vegetable family, all of which are known for their anti-oxidant and anti-inflammatory properties.

SERVES 1

GRILLED ASPARAGUS WITH LEMON CREAM

Time to try... AI diet

Ingredients

- 1 tbsp olive oil
- ¼ tsp Himalayan sea salt
- 1 tsp fresh dill, shredded
- 6 spears of asparagus
- ½ avocado
- 1 tbsp coconut yoghurt
- 1 lemon, zest only
- 1 tbsp fresh dill fronds extra to serve

Method

1 Pre-heat the grill.

2 Mix the olive oil with the salt and dill.

3 Remove any thick fibrous parts from the asparagus spears.

4 Brush the oil over the asparagus and place under a hot grill and cook for 6-7 minutes, turning half way through.

5 Peel and de-stone from the avocado. Scoop out the flesh and mash with a fork until really smooth.

6 Mix the coconut yoghurt into the avocado and add the lemon zest.

7 Place the grilled asparagus on to a plate and top with the avocaco and lemon cream.

8 Decorate with a little extra fresh dill.

CHEF'S NOTE

You could use either the green or purple variety of asparagus for this dish but try to avoid the white one; they are grown in the dark and don't have the same rich beneficial phytochemicals.

SERVES 1

SUMMER HERB BOWL AND MUSTARD DRIZZLE

Time to try.... AI diet

Ingredients

- 150g/5oz rocket leaves
- 75g/3oz baby spinach leaves
- 1 small bunch of flat leaf parsley
- 1 small bunch of chives
- 1 tbsp fresh oregano leaves, chopped
- 1 tbsp fresh mint leaves, chopped
- Small handful of wild garlic (optional, if it's available)
- 1 tbsp avocado oil
- 1 tsp organic Dijon mustard
- 1 tsp maple syrup
- 2 tbsp apple cider vinegar

Method

1. Place the rocket leaves and spinach leaves onto a plate.
2. Chop the parsley and chives and mix up with the leaves on the plate.
3. Sprinkle over the oregano and mint and the wild garlic, if using.
4. Mix the avocado oil with the mustard, maple syrup and vinegar.
5. Drizzle over 1-2 tbsps of the mustard drizzle, leaving any excess for another day.

CHEF'S NOTE

Make sure you use the apple cider vinegar variety that has no added yeast.

SERVES 1

STRAWBERRY FIELDS

Time to try....
AI diet

Ingredients

- 5 strawberries, hulled and sliced
- 1 tbsp fresh mint leaves
- ½ medium cucumber
- ½ avocado
- 175g/6oz baby spinach leaves
- 75g/3oz rocket leaves
- 1 tbsp olive oil
- 1 tbsp balsamic vinegar
- ½ lemon juice
- Pinch of Himalayan sea salt

Method

1 Place the strawberries and mint into a bowl.

2 Halve and slice the cucumber, leaving the skin and seeds intact.

3 Peel and remove the stone from the avocado and slice the flesh.

4 Mix the olive oil, balsamic, lemon juice and salt together.

5 Add the cucumber, avocado and salad leaves to the strawberries and toss together.

6 Tip onto a plate and drizzle over the dressing.

CHEF'S NOTE

It is better to make your own dressings for salads as most shop brought varieties have added black pepper, which needs to be avoided.

SERVES 1

SUNDAY VEG BOWL

Time to try... AI diet

Ingredients

- 1 tsp olive oil
- 3 cavolo nero leaves, shredded
- 3 green cabbage leaves, shredded
- Handful of kale, shredded, tough stalks removed
- ½ a leek, chopped
- 1 garlic clove, crushed

For The Drizzle

- 1 tbsp olive oil
- 1 tsp onion powder
- ½ tbsp balsamic vinegar
- ½ tbsp coconut aminos

Method

1 Heat the oil in a frying pan or wok.

2 Add the cavolo nero, cabbage, kale, leek and garlic and stir fry for 5-6 minutes, until the greens have wilted.

3 Stir the drizzle ingredients into the pan and cook for a further 1-2 minutes to heat through.

4 Serve immediately.

CHEF'S NOTE

Cavolo nero is one of the darkest green brassica vegetables and a rich source of beta-carotenes.

SERVES 1

SPICED CHICKEN FLATBREAD

Time to try.... AI diet

Ingredients

For The Flatbread

- 125g/4oz tapioca starch
- 4 tbsp coconut flour
- 1 tsp onion powder
- 1 tsp cream of tartar
- ½ tsp baking powder
- 2 tbsp olive oil
- 120-150ml/4-5floz of warm water

For The Chicken

- 1 onion, halved and sliced
- 1 large handful of cooked chicken breast, shredded
- 1 tsp olive oil
- 1 tsp ground ginger
- ½ tsp ground cinnamon
- ½ tsp turmeric
- Handful of rocket leaves

Method

1 Pre-heat the oven to 400°F/200°C/Gas Mark 6 and line a baking tray.

2 Mix the tapioca starch with the coconut flour, onion powder, cream of tartar and baking powder.

3 Pour in the olive oil and enough warm water to make a crumbly dough.

4 Press on a to the baking tray and roll flat to create a circle.

5 Bake in the oven for 10-15 minutes until cooked.

6 Meanwhile, heat the oil in a saucepan and add the sliced onion. Stir and cook over a low heat for 10 minutes, until caramelised and sweet.

7 Stir in the chicken and spices and cook for a further 2 minutes to heat through.

8 Put the rocket on top of the flatbread and top with the chicken mix.

CHEF'S NOTE

Arrowroot may be used in replacement of the tapioca starch if you prefer.

SERVES 1

SPICED RAW CAULIFLOWER

Time to try....
AI diet

Ingredients

- 200g/7oz cauliflower, chopped into mini florets
- 2 tbsp flat leaf parsley, chopped
- 2 tbsp fresh oregano, chopped
- 1 tbsp fresh coriander/cilantro, chopped
- 1 tbsp pomegranate seeds
- 2 tbsp coconut oil, melted
- ½ tsp ground ginger
- ½ tsp ground cinnamon
- ½ tsp turmeric
- Pinch of Himalayan sea salt

Method

1. Mix the cauliflower, parsley, oregano, coriander/cilantro and pomegranate seeds together.
2. Mix the coconut oil, spices and salt together and pour over the cauliflower.
3. Leave to soak for an hour if possible before serving, to allow the flavours to develop and penetrate the cauliflower.

CHEF'S NOTE

Pomegranates are full of vitamin C and a great addition as they add some welcome texture and crunch to a dish.

SERVES 1

TUNA AND RED ONION PACKED LUNCH

Time to try.... AI diet

Ingredients

- 125g/4oz tin of tinned tuna
- 1 small red onion, halved and sliced
- 1 tsp olive oil
- 1 tbsp lemon zest
- Pinch of Himalayan sea salt
- ½ avocado
- ¼ iceberg lettuce, shredded
- 1 red apple
- 1 tbsp lemon juice

Method

1 Drain the tuna and flake evenly. Stir through the onions, olive oil, lemon zest and salt.

2 Place at one end of a plastic lunch box.

3 Peel and remove the stone from the avocado and slice. Place in a line next to the tuna.

4 Add the shredded lettuce to the container next to the avocado.

5 Wash, core and slice the apple. Mix with the lemon juice to prevent it from browning.

6 Place the apple next to the lettuce.

7 Put the lid on and pack a fork.

CHEF'S NOTE

Tinned tuna is a tasty protein to add to a meal, but try and make sure you purchase the "line caught" tuna.

Time to try....

AUTOIMMUNE

DINNER

SERVES 1

PORK GRILLED & PINEAPPLE AND BOWL

Time to try... AI diet

Ingredients

- ½ small pineapple, cut into wedges
- 1 tbsp olive oil
- 1 tsp raw honey
- 1 pork loin steak
- 1 handful of rocket leaves
- 1 celery stalk, sliced
- ¼ cucumber
- 1 tbsp avocado oil
- 1 tbsp lemon juice
- 1 tbsp flat leaf parsley, chopped
- ¼ tsp pink Himalayan sea salt

Method

1 Heat a griddle pan until scorching hot.

2 Mix the olive oil and honey together and brush over both sides of the pork.

3 Griddle the pork on both sides for 7-8 minutes, until charred, caramelized and cooked.

4 Add the pineapple to the pan and cook for 1-2 minutes on both sides.

5 Place the rocket, celery and cucumber in a bowl.

6 Slice the pork and put into the bowl with the salad, parsley and pineapple.

7 Mix the salt, avocado oil and lemon juice together and drizzle over the top.

8 Serve immediately.

CHEF'S NOTE

Avocado oil is a great base for a salad dressing as it has a mild sweet and nutty flavour and also provides protective carotenoids.

SERVES 4

TUNA AND CARAMELISED ONION PIZZA

Time to try... AI diet

Ingredients

For The Pizza Base
- 85g/3oz arrowroot starch
- 4 tbsp coconut flour
- 1 tsp cream of tartar
- ½ tsp baking powder
- ½ tsp pink Himalayan sea salt
- 2 tbsp olive oil
- 120ml/4floz warm water

For The Topping
- 1 tbsp olive oil
- 2 red onion, halved and sliced
- 200g/7oz tin of tuna
- 7-8 black olives, chopped
- 150g/5oz rocket leaves
- Small bunch of flat leaf parsley
- Small bunch of fresh oregano
- 4-5 fresh basil leaves
- 3 tbsp olive oil
- 2 tbsp lemon juice

Method

1 Mix the pizza base ingredients together until a firm dough is formed.

2 Press down onto the baking tray, forming a circle.

3 Bake in the oven for 15-20 minutes, until golden and cooked.

4 In a frying pan, add the onions and oil and heat over a medium heat for 8-10 minutes. Stir until softened and sweet.

5 Add the tuna and olives to the pan and stir until the tuna is broken up and everything is well combined.

6 Place the herbs oil and lemon juice into a blender and process until smooth.

7 To serve, place the pizza base on a board, scatter over the rocket leaves. Add the tuna mix and drizzle over the herb oil.

8 Cut in to 4 wedges.

CHEF'S NOTE

Olives contain vitamin E and lots of iron and also add a tasty, salty flavour to a dish without having to add any extra seasoning.

SERVES 1

PORK, SWEET POTATO AND APPLE BAKE

Time to try... AI diet

Ingredients

- 1 small sweet potato
- 1 boneless pork chop
- 4 sage leaves, roughly chopped
- 1 red skinned apple, cored and sliced
- ½ tsp pink Himalayan sea salt
- 1 tbsp olive oil
- 4-5 florets of broccoli

Method

1 Pre-heat the oven to 375°F/190°C/Gas Mark 5 and grease a small casserole dish.

2 Cut the sweet potato in to wedges and put into the casserole dish.

3 Scatter over the apple pieces and sage leaves and season with the salt.

4 Place the pork chop on top and drizzle the olive oil over.

5 Bake in the oven for 20-25 minutes until the potato is soft and the pork cooked through.

6 Steam or boil the broccoli and serve immediately.

CHEF'S NOTE

Pork contains useful levels of zinc, which supports healthy immune functions.

SERVES 2

PORK CHOPS WITH MANGO RELISH

Time to try.... AI diet

Ingredients

- 2 pork chops
- Zest and juice of 1 orange
- 1 tbsp rosemary leaves
- 1 tbsp coconut aminos
- 1 tbsp coconut oil, melted

For The Mango Relish

- ½ cucumber, finely diced
- 1 red onion, halved and finely diced
- 1 mango, peeled and stone removed, and finely diced
- Medium bunch of coriander/ cilantro, chopped
- 1 tbsp olive oil
- ½ avocado, peeled, de-stoned and finely diced
- ¼ tsp pink Himalayan sea salt
- 4-5 sliced radishes to serve

Method

1 Mix the pork chops with the orange zest, juice, rosemary leaves, coconut aminos and coconut oil. Leave to marinade in a non-metallic bowl for 24 ours if possible.

2 When ready to serve, heat grill to a medium heat and place the pork under. Cook for 9-10 minutes on both sides, until cooked through.

3 Meanwhile, mix all of the other ingredients together for the mango relish.

4 Put one pork chop on a plate and spoon over half of the relish.

5 Top with the sliced radishes and repeat with the other plate.

CHEF'S NOTE

Mangoes contain stomach soothing enzymes and have been used as an ingredient to treat digestive issues for centuries.

SERVES 2

MEATBALLS AND COURGETTI

Time to try.... AI diet

Ingredients

- 2 tbsp olive oil
- 1 white onion, finely diced
- 3 garlic cloves, crushed
- ¼ tsp pink Himalayan sea salt
- 1 tbsp dried oregano
- 300g/11oz beef mince
- ½ fennel bulb, shredded
- 1 tbsp gelatine +4 tbsp hot water
- 1 red onion, halved and sliced
- 8 chestnut mushrooms, sliced
- 300g/11oz courgette noodles (courgettes/zucchini spiralized)

Method

1 Heat the 1 tbsp oil for the meatballs in a frying pan and add the white onion and 1 garlic clove. Cook for 4-5 minutes until softened. Leave to cool a little.

2 In a bowl, add the oregano, salt and minced beef.

3 Mix the gelatine with the hot water and whisk hard for 1-2 minutes until frothy.

4 Mix the mince, gelatine and cooled onions and garlic. With damp hands, roll in to 10 balls.

5 In the same frying pan, add the rest of the oil and gently heat. Add the red onion, fennel and 2 garlic cloves and cook until softened.

6 Add the mushrooms and cook over a high heat to release the juices.

7 Add the meatballs to the pan and cook over a high heat to brown.

8 Cook for 15-20 minutes over a medium heat, until the meatballs are cooked through.

9 Add the courgette to the pan and stir for 2-3 minutes to coat in the oils and soften a little.

10 Divide between 2 plates and serve immediately.

CHEF'S NOTE

Vegetables that have been spiralized are a great aid for an Autoimmune Diet eating plan. They can replace pasta and noodles quite easily and they're full of plant nutrition.

SERVES 2

PRAWN AND ASPARAGUS "RISOTTO"

Time to try....
AI diet

Ingredients

- 1 tsp olive oil
- 1 onion, diced
- 1 garlic clove, crushed
- 1 large cauliflower
- 5-6 spears of asparagus, chopped
- ¼ pink Himalayan sea salt
- 200g/7oz cooked prawns
- 1 lemon, juice and zest
- 150g/5oz watercress, thick stalks removed

Method

1 Heat the oil in a large frying pan or wok. Add the onion and garlic and cook over a medium heat for 4-5 minutes until softened

2 Process the cauliflower in a blender until it resembles rice grains.

3 Add the cauliflower and the asparagus to the pan and stir fry for 4-5 minutes until softened, but still with a little bite.

4 Add the salt, prawns, lemon juice and zest and cook until the prawns are heated through.

5 Divide between 2 plates and top with the watercress.

CHEF'S NOTE

Prawns are a quick dinner time ingredient that are full of protein and B vitamins, crucial for metabolism and cell function.

SERVES 2

BAKED POTATOES WITH CHICKEN LIVER

Time to try... AI diet

Ingredients

- 2 medium sweet potatoes, baked
- 1 tbsp olive oil
- 1 carrot, chopped finely
- 1 celery stalk, chopped finely
- 1 onion, chopped finely
- 1 garlic clove
- 300g/11oz chicken livers
- 300ml beef bone broth
- 1 tbsp coconut aminos
- 1 bay leaf
- 1 tbsp rosemary leaves, chopped
- 200g/7oz spinach leaves, steamed

Method

1 Heat the oil in a frying pan and add the carrot, celery, onion and garlic and cook over a medium heat for 5-6 minutes, until softened.

2 Turn the heat up and add the chicken livers. Cook for 10 minutes until browned.

3 Pour over the bone broth, coconut aminos, bay leaf and rosemary leaves.

4 Simmer for 10 minutes until thickened a little and livers cooked.

5 Serve immediately, spooned on top of the sweet potatoes with some steamed spinach.

CHEF'S NOTE

When following an Autoimmune Diet eating plan, it is really worthwhile trying to eat one serving of organ meat once a week. Chicken livers are full of flavour and very cheap!

SERVES 2

COD LAKSA

Time to try....
AI diet

Ingredients

- 1 onion, finely diced
- 1 tbsp grated fresh ginger root
- 1 stalk of lemongrass, chopped roughly
- 1 tbsp coconut oil
- 1 tsp turmeric
- 1 garlic clove, crushed
- 600ml/1 pint coconut milk
- 450ml/15½floz chicken stock
- 2 pak choi, leaves sliced lengthways
- 200g/7oz courgette noodles
- 2 large cod fillets
- 1 tbsp shredded lime zest and 2 tbsp chopped fresh coriander/cilantro to serve
- 3 spring onions, shredded

Method

1 To make the laksa base, put the onion, ginger and lemongrass into a blender and process until smooth.

2 Add the coconut oil to a saucepan and add the garlic. Cook briefly over a gentle heat.

3 Add the onion base and cook for 4-5 minutes to soften and allow the flavours to release.

4 Add the coconut milk, stock and turmeric and simmer gently for 10 minutes, adding the pak choi and courgette noodles towards the end.

5 Pour water in to a deep pan and poach the cod for 7-8 minutes until cooked and just flaking.

6 Put the fillets into 2 bowls.

7 Tip over the coconut laksa liquid, ensuring the vegetables are equal.

8 Top with the spring onion, shredded lime zest and fresh coriander/cilantro.

CHEF'S NOTE

The diuretic effect of lemongrass assists the kidneys in removing toxins, by increased urination, working as a great anti-oxidant.

SERVES 2

ROAST CHICKEN WITH SALSA VERDE

Time to try... AI diet

Ingredients

- 1 tbsp olive oil
- 4 chicken thighs
- 8 garlic cloves
- 1 lemon, cut in to wedges
- 1 tsp pink Himalayan sea salt

For The Salsa Verde

- 1 large bunch of flat leaf parsley
- 1 small bunch of fresh oregano
- 5-6 leaves of fresh basil
- 5-6 leaves of fresh mint leaves
- 1 tbsp capers
- 4 anchovy fillets
- 2 tbsp red wine vinegar
- 6 tbsp olive oil
- 1 garlic clove
- Steamed cauliflower and broccoli to serve

Method

1 Pre-heat the oven to 400°F/200°C/Gas Mark 6 and grease a small baking dish.

2 Add the chicken thighs, garlic cloves, olive oil and lemon wedges and mix well to combine.

3 Roast in the oven for 45 minutes, until the chicken thighs are cooked through (check the juices run clear from the thickest part).

4 Place all of the salsa verde ingredients in to a food processor and blend until smooth (or leave a little chunky if you prefer).

5 When the chicken is cooked, divide between 2 plates, add the steamed vegetables and spoon over the salsa verde.

CHEF'S NOTE

This salsa verde is a source of protein and omega-3 from the anchovies. They add a lovely saltiness and can be used to enhance many savoury dishes.

SERVES 2

SPRING VEGETABLES AND HERB CHICKEN

Time to try...
AI diet

Ingredients

- 4 chicken thighs
- 1 litre/1½ pints of chicken bone broth/stock
- 1 red onion, diced
- 2 garlic cloves, sliced
- 1 small bunch of flat leaf parsley
- 2 sprigs of lemon thyme
- 2 sprigs of marjoram
- 2 carrots, sliced thickly on the diagonal
- 1 celery stalk, sliced
- 1 lemon, zest only
- 150g/5oz asparagus spears, trimmed
- 150g/5oz broccoli florets, chopped
- ¼ savoy cabbage, shredded

Method

1 Put the chicken in a large lidded saucepan and add the chicken stock or bone broth. Add the onion, garlic, herbs, celery and carrots and bring to a boil.

2 Simmer with a lid on for 45 minutes, until the chicken is cooked and fall ng off the bones.

3 Add the lemon zest, asparagus, broccoli and cabbage to the pan and simmer for a further 5-6 minutes until softened.

4 Turn off the heat and leave to cool a little.

5 Remove the chicken and strip meat from the bones. Divide the meat between 2 bowls.

6 Pour over some of the broth and divide the vegetables between them.

CHEF'S NOTE

Use organic, pasture fed chicken for the best nutrition. Avoiding protein that has been treated with unnecessary medication is essential to reduce toxins in our diets.

SERVES 1

BRAISED TURKEY WITH GREMOLATA

Time to try....
AI diet

Ingredients

- 1 tbsp olive oil
- 1 small turkey escalope
- 1 small onion, diced
- 1 celery stick, sliced
- 1 small carrot, diced
- 300ml/10½floz vegetable stock
- 1 bay leaf
- 2 tbsp fresh thyme, chopped
- 100g/3½oz chestnut mushrooms, sliced

Gremolata

- 1 tbsp flat leaf parsley, chopped
- 1 tbsp lemon zest
- 1 garlic clove
- ½ tsp pink Himalayan sea salt

Method

1 Heat the olive oil in a saucepan and add the turkey escalope and brown all over. Add the onion, carrot, celery thyme, bay leaf, stock and mushrooms.

2 Bring to a boil and place on a lid.

3 Simmer for 8-10 minutes until the turkey is cooked through.

4 Place the turkey and vegetables on to a deep plate. Spoon over a bit of the stock.

5 Roughly chop all of the ingredients together for the gremolata until quite fine. Sprinkle over the turkey and serve immediately.

CHEF'S NOTE

Turkey is high in selenium, which is a great anti-oxidant and provides happy hormones for a good mood.

SERVES 3

VENISON AND CRANBERRY HOT POT

Time to try... AI diet

Ingredients

- 1 tbsp olive oil
- 500g/1lb 2oz venison steak, cubed
- 1 onion, diced
- 1 garlic clove, crushed
- 2 carrots, diced
- 1 celery stalk, diced
- 1 tbsp fresh tarragon leaves, chopped
- 150g/5oz chestnut mushrooms, sliced
- 300ml vegetable stock
- ½ pink Himalayan sea salt
- 100g/3½oz fresh or frozen cranberries
- 1 tbsp gelatine + 4 tbsp hot water
- Steamed kale to serve

Method

1 Pre-heat the oven to 350°F/180°C/Gas Mark 4.

2 Heat the oil in a casserole dish and add the venison. Cook over a high heat until brown all over.

3 Add the onion, garlic, carrots and celery and stir over a medium heat for 5-6 minutes until softened.

4 Add the tarragon, mushrooms, stock, cranberries and salt and bring to a simmer.

5 Whisk the gelatine with the hot water and 1-2 minutes until frothy. Add to the casserole dish.

6 Place the casserole, covered, into the oven and cook for 1-1½ hours.

7 Serve with the steamed kale.

CHEF'S NOTE

Cranberries are antibacterial and commonly used to help prevent infections in the urinary tract, bladder and kidneys.

SERVES 1

GRILLED MACKEREL, APPLES & SAUERKRAUT

Time to try... AI diet

Ingredients

- 2 small mackerel fillets, skin on
- 2 tsp olive oil
- 1 small bunch of parsley
- 1 garlic clove
- 1 celery stalk
- 1 tbsp lemon zest
- 1 tbsp lemon juice
- 1 tsp fresh ginger root, grated
- ¼ tsp pink Himalayan sea salt
- 2 tbsp sauerkraut
- 1 eating apple
- 1 tsp coconut aminos

Method

1. Place the mackerel fillets in a non-metallic bowl.
2. Add the celery, parsley, garlic, lemon zest, juice and salt in to a food processor and blend until smooth. Pour over the mackerel and leave to marinade for at least 2 hours.
3. When ready to cook, heat the grill to high and cook the mackerel on both sides for 3-4 minutes until crisp and cooked.
4. Core and slice the apple and mix with the sauerkraut.
5. Place onto a plate and top with the mackerel fillets.

CHEF'S NOTE

Mackerel is an easy to cook oily fish, full of omega-3. Aim to eat fish or shellfish 3 times a week when following an Autoimmune Diet eating plan.

SERVES 1

LIVER, ONION AND "MASH"

Time to try... AI diet

Ingredients

- 1 tbsp olive oil
- 1 tbsp coconut flour
- 150g/5oz of lamb's liver
- 1 onion, halved and sliced
- 120ml/4floz bone broth/stock
- 1 tbsp flat leaf parsley, chopped
- 1 medium cauliflower head, cut in chunks
- 1 tbsp coconut milk
- 1 tsp gelatine
- ½ tsp pink Himalayan sea salt

Method

1. Heat the oil in a large frying pan.
2. Dust the liver with the flour and add to the pan. Fry over a high heat to brown all over for 3-4 minutes.
3. Add the onion slices and cook for a further 4-5 minutes to soften the onions.
4. Add the stock or bone broth and bring to a simmer.
5. Cook for a further 5 minutes and add the parsley.
6. Meanwhile, steam the cauliflower until soft.
7. Add to a blender and process. Whilst running add the gelatine and coconut milk (add extra to get the right consistency if necessary).
8. Add the salt and place onto a plate.
9. Top with the cocked liver, onion and pan juices.

CHEF'S NOTE

Try to include offal/organ meet to your diet once a week. Some cuts, like liver are really cheap and will add vital vitamin B12 to your diet.

SERVES 1

GARLIC AND LEMON KEBABS

Time to try... AI diet

Ingredients

- 2 tbsp coconut oil, melted
- 1 tbsp lemon zest
- 1 tsp raw honey
- 1 garlic clove, crushed
- 1 tbsp flat leaf parsley, chopped
- 1 courgette/zucchini, cut in to chunks
- 1 chicken breast or 1 pork fillet, chopped in mouth sized chunks
- 6 mushrooms, halved
- 1 handful of shredded iceberg
- ¼ cucumber, sliced

Method

1 Pre-heat the grill.

2 Mix the coconut oil, lemon zest, honey, garlic and parsley together.

3 Thread the pork or chicken on to skewers, alternating with the courgette/zucchini chunks and mushroom halves.

4 Brush the coconut oil mix on to the kebabs, all over. Place under a hot grill on a baking sheet and cook over a medium heat, brushing more oil on if necessary.

5 Turn over after 6-7 minutes and cook the same time again, to ensure the meat is cooked and the vegetables softened.

6 Place the shredded iceberg and cucumber on a plate and add the cooked kebabs.

CHEF'S NOTE

Make sure you always use raw honey as this is unprocessed and unheated, still keeping all of the anti-microbial and immune boosting properties found in this natural sweetener.

SERVES 2

LAMB AND CAULIFLOWER 'RICE'

Time to try... AI diet

Ingredients

- 2 garlic cloves
- 1 lemongrass stalk
- 1 thumb size piece fresh root ginger
- 1 tsp turmeric
- 1 tsp ground cinnamon
- 1 bunch fresh coriander
- 2 tbsp + 1 tsp olive oil
- 300g/11oz lamb fillet, cut into chunks
- 2 onions, sliced
- 1 courgette/zucchini, sliced diagonally
- 300ml/10½floz bone broth/meat stock
- 1 tbsp gelatine + 4 tbsp water)
- 1 tbsp coconut cream
- 200g/7oz spinach leaves
- 1 medium head of cauliflower
- 1 tbsp coconut oil, melted
- ½ tsp pink Himalayan sea salt

Method

1 Place the garlic, lemongrass, ginger, turmeric, cinnamon, most of the coriander and 2 tbsp olive oil in a blender. Process until smooth.

2 Heat the 1 tsp olive oil in a frying pan and add the lamb chunks. Cook over a high heat for 4-5 minutes to brown all over.

3 Add the garlic paste from the blender and stir well to coat the lamb. Cook for a further 3-4 minutes.

4 Add the onion and continue to cook for a further 4-5 minutes until soft. Add the courgette/zucchini slices and stock and bring to a simmer.

5 Mix the gelatine with the water and whisk for 1-2 minutes until frothy.

6 Pour in to the lamb mix and cook for a further 10 minutes to thicken and cook the lamb.

7 Stir in the coconut cream and spinach and remove from the heat (the spinach should wilt in the heat).

8 Process the cauliflower in a blender until it resembles rice.

9 Heat the coconut oil in a frying pan and add the cauliflower and salt. Heat for 4-5 minutes until the cauliflower is soft.

10 Divide the cauliflower between 2 plates and top with the lamb mix.

11 Scatter over the reaming chopped coriander/ cilantro to serve

Time to try....

AUTOIMMUNE

DESSERT

SERVES 1

BAKED APPLES WITH CINNAMON CRUNCH

Time to try....
AI diet

Ingredients

- 1 apple, cored
- ½ tsp ground cinnamon
- 1 tbsp coconut flour
- 2 tbsp coconut butter
- 1 tbsp maple syrup
- Coconut cream, whipped, to serve (see tip)

Method

1. Pre-heat the oven to 400˚F/200˚C/Gas Mark 6 and grease a small casserole dish.
2. Place the apple in the dish.
3. Mix the cinnamon, flour and butter together and create a lump texture.
4. Stuff some of this into the centre of the apple where the core was and sprinkle the rest over the apple.
5. Pour the maple syrup over the top and bake in the oven for 35-40 minutes until the apple is soft and oozing.
6. Serve with whipped coconut cream.

CHEF'S NOTE

Whipped coconut cream is a lovely treat. If you leave a full fat tin of coconut milk in the fridge, you should be able to spoon off the separated thick top and whip it up with a whisk. Use the thinner milk to add to smoothies.

SERVES 6

BANANA BREAD PUDDING WITH CACAO NIBS

Time to try.... AI diet

Ingredients

- 1 tbsp gelatine + 4tbsp hot water
- 125g/4oz tigernut flour
- 75g/3oz tapioca starch
- 1 tsp ground cinnamon
- 4 tbsp coconut sugar
- 1 tsp baking powder
- 120ml/4floz coconut milk
- 2 bananas, peeled and mashed
- 3 tbsp cacao nibs
- Fresh fruit and coconut yoghurt to serve if desired

Method

1 Pre-heat the oven to 400°F/200°C/Gas Mark 6 and grease a small loaf tin.

2 Mix the gelatine with the water and whisk well for 1-2 minutes until frothy.

3 In a bowl, add the tigernut flour, tapioca, cinnamon, sugar, baking powder and cacao nibs.

4 Stir the bananas into the milk and add to the dry ingredients.

5 Beat in the gelatine mix and place in the loaf tin.

6 Level it off and bake in the oven for 30-35 minutes or until risen and cooked through.

7 Serve with fresh fruit and coconut yoghurt if desired.

CHEF'S NOTE

Tigernut flour is one of the only flours available on an Autoimmune Diet diet. It's made from a tuber, similar to yams and adds a lovely sweetness to bakes.

SERVES 2

MANGO ICE WITH MINT CRUNCH

Time to try....
AI diet

Ingredients

- 300g/11oz frozen mango chunks
- 120ml/4floz of coconut water
- 1 tbsp lime juice
- 1 tbsp lime zest
- 1 tsp raw honey
- 2 tbsp coconut sugar
- 7-8 fresh mint leaves

Method

1 On a board spread the mint leaves and coconut sugar, and chop. Mix until you have a coarse and sugary, minty blend.

2 Put the mango, coconut water, lime juice and zest and honey into a blender and process until smooth.

3 Scoop into two glasses and top with the mint sugar.

4 Serve immediately.

CHEF'S NOTE

Limes are considered low oxalate and can be helpful for those who are susceptible to developing kidney stones.

SERVES 2

PEAR CRUNCH

Time to try...
AI diet

Ingredients

- 3 pears, peeled, cored and sliced
- 1 tbsp maple syrup
- ½ tsp ground cinnamon
- ½ tsp ground ginger
- 4 tbsp coconut flour
- 1 tbsp coconut sugar
- 2 tbsp coconut flakes
- 1 tbsp coconut butter
- 2 tbsp coconut oil, melted

Method

1 Pre-heat the oven to 400°F/200°C/Gas Mark 6 and grease a small casserole dish.

2 Place the pears into the dish and mix well with the maple syrup and ground cinnamon.

3 In a bowl, add the coconut flour, sugar, ginger and coconut oil and flakes. Stir well and clump together to make a crumbly mix. Add a little water if this is still slightly dry.

4 Spoon the crumble mix on top of the pears.

5 Bake in the oven for 20-25 minutes, until the top is crunchy and the pears soft.

CHEF'S NOTE

This dessert uses a lot of coconut products – these are anti-inflammatory, metabolism boosting and hormone balancing.

BANANA AND BERRY ICE

SERVES 2

Time to try.... AI diet

Ingredients

- 2 bananas, peeled, chopped and frozen
- 200g/7oz frozen fruits of the forest (cherries, blackberries, etc.)
- 1 tbsp coconut milk
- 1 tbsp maple syrup
- 1 tbsp collagen powder
- 2 tbsp coconut flakes, toasted

Method

1 Place all of the ingredients except the collagen, into a blender and process until smooth.

2 Add the collagen and continue to process until light and whipped.

3 Divide between 2 glasses and serve with the toasted coconut flakes.

CHEF'S NOTE

Bananas are a great source of potassium, essential for heart muscle health and fluid balancing.

RASPBERRY SHORTCAKE

SERVES 2

Time to try... AI diet

Ingredients

- 150g/5oz raspberries
- 1 tbsp maple syrup
- 125g/4oz cassava flour
- ¾ tsp baking powder
- 1 tbsp coconut sugar
- 40g/1½oz lard, fridge cold
- 4 tbsp coconut yoghurt

Method

1 Pre-heat the oven to 400°F/200°C/Gas Mark 6 and grease a baking tray.

2 Add the raspberries to a saucepan with the maple syrup. Heat gently to break down the berries to make a raspberry syrup. Leave to cool.

3 Mix the flour, baking powder and sugar together and cut the lard into the dry ingredients with a knife.

4 When the flour and lard are like breadcrumbs, add enough cold water to make a firm dough.

5 Shape into 2 rounds and press down lightly onto the baking tray.

6 Bake for 15-20 minutes or until risen and coloured.

7 Allow to cool and then slice each shortcake in half.

8 Add two halves to a plate, top each with 1 tbsp of yoghurt and drizzle over the raspberry syrup.

CHEF'S NOTE

Raspberries are a great source of anthocyanidins, which act as powerful anti-oxidants.

SERVES 9

AUTOIMMUNE BROWNIE

Time to try... AI diet

Ingredients

- 1 tbsp gelatine + 5 tbsp hot water
- 120ml/4floz coconut oil
- 4 tbsp maple syrup
- 4 tbsp raw cacao powder
- 125g/4½oz tigernut flour
- 3 tbsp arrowroot starch
- 1 tsp baking powder

Method

1 Pre-heat the oven to 400°F/200°C/Gas Mark 6 and grease an 8"x8" baking tin.

2 Mix the gelatine with the hot water and whisk for 1-2 minutes, until frothy.

3 Add the maple syrup and coconut oil to the gelatine and mix well.

4 Put the cacao powder, tigernut flour, arrowroot and baking powder in a bowl and add the gelatine mix.

5 Beat well until combined.

6 Pour into the prepared tin and bake for 15-20 minutes until set on top but still lovely and squidgy underneath. You don't want to overcook this!

7 Cut in to 9 squares and serve warm or leave to cool.

CHEF'S NOTE

Use raw cacao powder here if you can. It provides better nutrition as the heating process removes the useful fatty acids, magnesium and iron it contains.

SERVES 4

BLUEBERRY COBBLER

Time to try... AI diet

Ingredients

- 300g/11oz blueberries
- 2 tbsp coconut oil, melted
- 3 tbsp coconut milk
- 25g/1oz arrowroot starch
- 25g/1oz coconut flour
- 1 tsp baking powder
- 1 tsp ground cinnamon
- 2 tbsp raw honey

Method

1 Pre-heat the oven to 400°F/200°C/Gas Mark 6 and grease a square baking tray, roughly 8"x8".

2 Scatter the blueberries all over the bottom of the tray.

3 Mix all of the cobbler ingredients together well and beat to combine.

4 Place spoonful's of the mix over the top of the blueberries (don't worry too much if some of the blueberries still show through).

5 Place in the oven for 20-25 minutes until golden and risen. Serve warm.

CHEF'S NOTE

Blueberries are full of vitamin C and fibre and also contain high levels of flavonoids, which are thought to prevent cell damage.

GOOSEBERRY AND GINGER GALETTE

SERVES 4

Time to try.... AI diet

Ingredients

- 250g/9oz gooseberries
- 4 tbsp coconut sugar
- 1 tsp fresh ginger root, grated 75g/3oz tigernut flour
- 75g/3oz arrowroot flour
- 25g/1oz coconut flour
- ½ tsp ground ginger
- 4 tbsp coconut oil, melted
- 1 tbsp coconut sugar
- Enough coconut milk to combine

Method

1 Pre-heat the oven to 400°F/200°C/Gas Mark 6 and grease a baking tray.

2 Halve the gooseberries and mix with the grated ginger and coconut sugar for the filling. Leave to one side.

3 In a bowl, add the flours, ground ginger, coconut sugar and coconut oil. Mix with enough coconut milk to make a firm dough.

4 Press the dough on the baking tray and shape into a rough circle.

5 Place the gooseberries on top, leaving a 2cm margin and bring the pastry up around the edges to seal.

6 Bake for 25-30 minutes until the crust is cooked and the gooseberries soft and oozing.

CHEF'S NOTE

Gooseberries are rich in vitamin C and help the body to absorb iron and to aid the formation of collagen.

SERVES 2

GRILLED BANANAS WITH PASSIONFRUIT DRIZZLE

Time to try... AI diet

Ingredients

- 2 large bananas
- 1 tsp ground cinnamon
- 2 passion fruit
- 1 tbsp maple syrup

Method

1 Pre-heat the grill.

2 Peel and slice the bananas in half, length ways,

3 Place onto a baking tray that fits under the grill.

4 Sprinkle on the cinnamon and grill for 3-4 minutes until toasted on top.

5 Halve the passion fruits and scoop out the flesh. Mix with the maple syrup.

6 Place 2 halves of the banana on a plate and drizzle over the passionfruit.

CHEF'S NOTE

Maple syrup is a good source of manganese, which is an essential mineral required for antioxidant defences. Use in moderation though as it's still a form of sweetener!

SERVES 2

BLACKBERRIES AND CREAM PARFAIT

Time to try... AI diet

Ingredients

- 150ml/5floz apple juice
- 2 tsp gelatine
- 200g/7oz coconut yoghurt
- 500g/1lb 2oz frozen blackberries/forest fruits
- 1 tsp maple syrup
- 1 tbsp toasted coconut flakes

Method

1 Heat the apple juice and bring to the boil. Whisk in the gelatine and stir until completely dissolved. Leave to cool.

2 Add the yoghurt and half of the fruit mix to a blender and process, pouring in the gelatine mix as it spins.

3 When combined, leave in the fridge to firm up.

4 Heat the remaining berries in the pan and add the syrup. Cook gently until they have broken down a little. Place in the fridge to cool.

5 When ready to serve, take 2 glasses and divide the yoghurt mix and fruit mix into layers.

6 Top with the coconut flakes.

CHEF'S NOTE

Blackberries are an excellent source of both soluble and insoluble fibre, great to promote good gut health.

SERVES 3-4

MINT CHOC ICE

Time to try... AI diet

Ingredients

- 2 avocados
- 250ml/9floz coconut milk
- ½ tsp peppermint extract
- Handful of fresh mint leaves
- 2 tbsp maple syrup
- 1 tbsp raw cacao powder

Method

1. Peel and remove the stones from the avocados.
2. Place all of the ingredients into a blender. Process until smooth.
3. Pour into a plastic container suitable for the freezer.
4. Freeze for 2 hours and give a good stir.
5. Freeze for a further 2 hours.
6. Leave to sit in the fridge for ½ hour before serving.

CHEF'S NOTE

Avocados are a wonderful way to add creaminess to a dessert or bake and will give you a boost of hormone balancing, vitamin E.

SERVES 4

GINGER AND APRICOT PUDDING

Time to try... AI diet

Ingredients

- 1 tbsp gelatine + 4 tbsp hot water
- 3 bananas, peeled and mashed
- 120ml/4floz of coconut oil, melted
- 120ml/4floz of raw honey
- 1 tsp ground ginger
- 60g/2½oz coconut flour
- 1 tsp baking powder
- 3 fresh apricots, de-stoned and sliced thinly
- Coconut yoghurt or cream to serve (optional)

Method

1 Pre-heat the oven to 375°F/190°C/Gas Mark 5 and grease a medium baking dish.

2 Mix the gelatine with the water and whisk until frothy.

3 Add all of the pudding ingredients together, apart from the apricots.

4 When well combined, add the apricots and gently stir in.

5 Pour into the baking dish and bake for 25-30 minutes until golden and risen.

6 Serve with coconut cream or yoghurt if desired.

CHEF'S NOTE

Apricots are rich in vitamin A and also associated with treating stomach issues, such as constipation.

SERVES 2

APPLE AND CINNAMON PUDDING

Time to try... AI diet

Ingredients

- 3 apples, peeled, cored and diced
- 1 tbsp coconut oil
- 3 tbsp maple syrup
- 3 tsp ground cinnamon
- 250ml/8½floz coconut milk
- ½ avocado, peeled and stone removed
- 1 tbsp gelatine + 3 tbsp hot water
- Whipped coconut cream and apple slices to serve

Method

1. Place the apples, coconut oil and syrup into a saucepan and cook over a medium heat.
2. When the apples have broken down and soft, add the cinnamon.
3. Using a blender or stick blender, process the apples until really smooth.
4. Add the avocado and mix again until smooth and combined.
5. Whisk in the coconut milk
6. Mix the gelatine with the water and whisk for 1-2 minutes until frothy.
7. Add the gelatine mix to the apple mix and pour equally into 2 glasses.
8. Store in the fridge for 2-3 hours to set.
9. Serve with a little whipped coconut cream and fresh apple slices on top.

CHEF'S NOTE

This mix could be used to fill an Autoimmune Diet pastry crust which has been pre-cooked. Store in the fridge and you have an apple tart!

SERVES 2

FRUIT KEBAB WITH LEMON AND BASIL DRESSING

Time to try... AI diet

Ingredients

- 4 slices of watermelon, cut into chunks
- 8 grapes
- 1 apple, cored and cut into chunks
- 8 small strawberries
- 1 banana, peeled and cut into chunks
- 4 tbsp lemon juice
- 1 tbsp raw honey
- 1 tbsp basil leaves, finely chopped

Method

1. Thread the fruit pieces onto skewers, alternating to separate the colours.
2. Mix the lemon juice, honey and basil leaves together to make a dressing.
3. Place the skewers onto 2 plates and drizzle over the dressing, ensuring all pieces of fruit are covered.
4. Serve immediately.

CHEF'S NOTE

Watermelon is a hydrating fruit to add to your diet. It contains Vitamin C and lycopene, both of which are useful for antioxidant protection and immune function boosting.

SERVES 2

PUMPKIN PANNA COTTA WITH STEWED PEARS

Time to try....
AI diet

Ingredients

- 1 tbsp gelatine + 3 tbsp hot water
- 400ml/14floz coconut milk
- 250ml/1 cup pumpkin puree
- 4 tbsp maple syrup
- 1 tsp ground cinnamon
- 2 pears, peeled, cored and sliced
- 1 tsp coconut oil
- 1 tbsp maple syrup
- 1 ground cinnamon

Method

1 Mix the gelatine with the hot water and whisk for 1-2 minutes until frothy.

2 Whisk the coconut milk, maple syrup and cinnamon together and add the gelatine mix.

3 Pour into 2 ramekins and place in the fridge for 3-4 hours until set.

4 Meanwhile place the pear pieces in a saucepan and add the oil, maple syrup and cinnamon. Cook over a medium heat until soft and cool in the fridge.

5 When ready to serve, place the ramekins on a plate and top with some of the stewed pear pieces.

CHEF'S NOTE

The essential oils found in cinnamon are considered to be helpful to treat a range of medical conditions, such as colds, asthma, insomnia, joint problems and digestive issues.

Time to try....

AUTOIMMUNE

SNACKS

SERVES 1

KIWI AND BANANA POWER SMOOTHIE

Time to try....
AI diet

Ingredients

- 1 banana, peeled and chopped
- 2 kiwis, peeled and sliced
- 1 tbsp collagen powder
- 200ml/7floz coconut milk
- 1 tsp flaxseed oil

Method

1 Place all of the ingredients into a high-speed blender.

2 Process until smooth.

3 Serve chilled with crushed ice if you wish.

CHEF'S NOTE

Kiwis are a great source of vitamin C, potassium, magnesium, copper and phosphorous.

SERVES 1

ELDERFLOWER AND GINGER SMOOTHIE

Time to try... AI diet

Ingredients

- ½ avocado, peeled and stone removed
- 250ml/8½floz coconut milk
- 1 elderflower head
- 1 apple, cored and cut into chunks
- 1 tsp fresh ginger root, grated

Method

1. Add the avocado, coconut milk, apple and ginger to a high-speed blender.
2. Pull the blossoms off the head of the elderflowers and add to the blender (do not add any stalks or leaves).
3. Process until all of the ingredients are smooth.
4. Serve immediately.

CHEF'S NOTE

When using elderflowers, be sure to only add the little blossoms to recipes as the stalks and leaves can produce some toxins.

SERVES 1

CUCUMBER, SPINACH AND APPLE QUENCHER

Time to try... AI diet

Ingredients

- ½ avocado, peeled and stone removed
- 250ml/8½floz coconut water
- ¼ cucumber
- 1 apple, cored and cut into chunks
- 1 handful of baby spinach leaves

Method

1 Add the avocado and coconut to a high-speed blender.

2 Roughly chop the cucumber, keeping seeds and skin intact.

3 Add the apple and cucumber to the blender with the spinach.

4 Process until smooth.

CHEF'S NOTE

Coconut water is considered to be one of the best forms of hydration and makes a great base for a refreshing drink to boost electrolyte sodium levels.

SERVES 1

PASSIONFRUIT AND MELON ENERGY DRINK

Time to try....
AI diet

Ingredients

- 1 passionfruit, halved and seeds removed
- 150g/5oz melon, sliced
- 250ml/8½floz coconut water
- 50g/2oz fresh pineapple chunks
- 1 tbsp coconut oil, melted
- ½ tsp fresh ginger root, grated

Method

1 Add all of the ingredients into a high-speed blender.

2 Process until all of the ingredients are smooth and pour into a chilled glass.

3 Serve with plenty of ice.

CHEF'S NOTE

Coconut oil is considered to have great anti-inflammatory and anti-oxidant properties and gives this drink a hit of energy.

SERVES 2

CINNAMON HOT CHOCOLATE

Time to try.... AI diet

Ingredients

- 400ml/14floz coconut milk
- 3 tbsp raw cacao powder
- 1 tbsp collagen powder
- ½ tsp ground cinnamon
- ½ tsp maple syrup

Method

1 Add all of the ingredients into a small saucepan.

2 Heat gently and bring to a boil.

3 Simmer for 4-5 minutes, whisking continually until thickened.

4 Pour into 2 heated mugs.

CHEF'S NOTE

Use collagen and not gelatine for drinks when adding this beneficial blend of amino-acids to drinks, as it won't form a gel and just thickens the drink.

SERVES 1

COCONUT FAT BOMB SMOOTHIE

Time to try.... AI diet

Ingredients

- 1 banana, peeled and chopped
- 250ml/8½floz coconut milk
- 1 tbsp coconut butter
- Handful of ice

Method

1 Place the banana, milk and butter into a high-speed blender and process until smooth.

2 Add the ice and whizz again.

3 Serve immediately.

CHEF'S NOTE

Coconut butter is a great ingredient to add to. It's rich in healthy fats and contains fibre and nutrients and helpful as an anti-inflammatory aid too.

SERVES 1

INDULGENT SPICED BROWNIE SMOOTHIE

Time to try.... AI diet

Ingredients

- 1 piece of Autoimmune brownie (from dessert section p72)
- 250ml/8½floz coconut milk
- ½ tsp ground cinnamon
- ½ banana, peeled and frozen
- ¼ tsp ground ginger

Method

1 Place all of the ingredients into a high-speed blender.

2 Process until everything is smooth.

3 Serve in a chilled glass as a treat.

CHEF'S NOTE

Using an Autoimmune friendly brownie in this creates luxury in a glass.

SERVES 1

BLUEBERRY, LIME AND MINT TONIC

Time to try... AI diet

Ingredients

- 150g/5oz blueberries
- 250ml/8½floz coconut water
- 1 tbsp lime juice
- 1 tsp raw honey
- 5-6 fresh mint leaves
- Large handful of ice

Method

1 Place all of the ingredients into a high-speed blender.

2 Process until the ingredients are smooth and the ice slushy.

3 Serve with lime wedges and extra mint leaves

CHEF'S NOTE

It is essential to stay hydrated regardless of what diet you follow. Creating tonics such as this will enable you to work towards reaching the recommended 8 glasses of fluid a day!

MAKES 8

GINGER AND COCONUT BOUNCE BALLS

Time to try....
AI diet

Ingredients

- 75g/3oz tigernut flour
- 25g/1oz coconut flour
- 1 tsp ground ginger
- 2 tbsp maple syrup
- 4 tbsp coconut oil, melted
- 1 tbsp collagen powder
- 2 tbsp desiccated coconut, to roll in

Method

1 Mix all of the ingredients together, apart from the desiccated coconut.

2 This should form a sticky dough, if not, add a little more maple syrup as this will depend on how absorbent your flours are.

3 Place the desiccated coconut on to a plate and roll the balls in it, to coat.

4 Place in the fridge to 'set' a little before serving.

CHEF'S NOTE

Coconut flour provides the body with lauric acid, which can help prevent infections and chronic diseases.

MAKES 20

GUMMY SWEETS

Time to try... AI diet

Ingredients

- Juice of 1 lemon
- 200g/7oz frozen berries (any sort)
- 1 tbsp maple syrup
- 25g/1oz gelatine powder
- 100ml/3½floz water

Method

1 Add the berries and lemon juice to a blender and process until smooth.

2 Pour the mix into a saucepan and add the maple syrup, gelatine and water.

3 Bring to a boil and remove from the heat.

4 If necessary, blend again to make sure the mix is smooth.

5 Pour into a lined 8"x8" square baking tin and place in the fridge for at least an hour to set.

6 Remove from the fridge and turn out onto a board. Cut into 20 squares.

CHEF'S NOTE

Berries are packed with anti-inflammatory polyphenols, to help support the growth of good gut bacteria.

KALE CRISPS

SERVES 2

Time to try.... AI diet

Ingredients

- 400g/14oz kale
- 1 tbsp coconut oil, melted
- 1 tsp garlic powder
- 1 tsp onion powder
- ¼ tsp pink Himalayan sea salt

Method

1 Pre-heat the oven to 350°F/180°C/Gas Mark 4 and grease a large baking tray.

2 Wash and remove the thick stalks from the kale. Dry with kitchen towel.

3 Massage the kale with the coconut oil, garlic and onion powder and the salt until thoroughly coated.

4 Spread onto the baking tray and bake in the oven for 10-15 minutes, or until crisp.

CHEF'S NOTE

Kale is an excellent source of vitamin C, fibre, anti-oxidants and vitamin K, all useful when following an Autoimmune Diet eating plan.

MAKES 9

HONEY COOKIES

Time to try... AI diet

Ingredients

- 2 tbsp avocado oil
- 2 tbsp raw honey
- 1 tbsp gelatine
- 50g/2oz coconut flour
- ¼ tsp baking powder

Method

1 Pre-heat the oven to 400°F/200°C/Gas Mark 6 and grease a large baking tray.

2 Mix the oil, honey and gelatine together and whisk until smooth.

3 Add the dry ingredients to the liquid and mix well.

4 Roll 9 balls from the dough (add a little water if your coconut flour is super absorbent!)

5 Flatten down on the baking tray and bake in the oven for 15-20 minutes.

6 When golden and cooked, cool on a rack.

CHEF'S NOTE

You could add some cacao nibs or dried fruit (in moderation) to the mix for variety.

SERVES 2

COURGETTE/ZUCCHINI CHIPS

Time to try.... AI diet

Ingredients

- 2 large courgettes/zucchini, cut into matchsticks
- 1 tbsp coconut oil, melted
- 1 tbsp coconut flour
- ½ tsp pink Himalayan sea salt
- 1 tbsp onion powder
- 1 tbsp dried oregano

Method

1 Pre-heat the oven to 400°F/200°C/Gas Mark 6 and grease a baking tray.

2 Mix the courgette/zucchini matchsticks with the oil, coconut flour, salt, onion powder and oregano.

3 Tip onto the baking tray and bake for 20-25 minutes until crisp.

4 Serve immediately.

CHEF'S NOTE

Courgettes/zucchini are full of vitamins C and K. This snack would make a great side dish for a main course.

26127256R00056

Printed in Great Britain
by Amazon

EIGHTY YEARS (CRAFT CARRIER

The first British aircraft carriers came into use at the outbreak of World War 1 in 1914. These were passenger packets quickly converted into seaplane carriers and were soon followed by the purpose built ARK ROYAL. There is an ARK ROYAL in today's Royal Navy. In the eighty years since 1914 the Navy has had 140 aircraft carriers of many sorts and sizes carrying many different aircraft. Some are famous ships and others are hardly remembered but all were faithfully served by the men who manned them and the aircraft squadron aircrews and groundcrews who used them. There have been many changes in the fortunes of the British Naval Aviation which has expanded in two world wars and been reduced in peacetime.

The Fleet Air Arm Museum has a unique collection of Naval aircraft and displays telling the history of the Fleet Air Arm. The "Carrier Experience" with its flight deck, aircraft and island recreates in sight and sound what it was like to be on a carrier in the 1970s with fixed wing jet aircraft and modern helicopters.

This book tells the story of the Royal Navy's aircraft carriers during the last eighty years and is a tribute to the ships, their aircraft and their crews. It has been written and produced by members of the Society of Friends of the Fleet Air Arm Museum and is one of the Society's contributions to the work of the Museum. The authors are grateful to the Museum Staff for all their help and encouragement particularly in finding photographs from the Museum's large collection.

Produced by

THE SOCIETY OF FRIENDS OF THE FLEET AIR ARM MUSEUM

The Society of Friends welcomes new members and details can be obtained from:
The Fleet Air Arm Museum, Box D.6. R.N.A.S. Yeovilton. Somerset. BA22 8H.

First Published by
The Society of Friends
of the
Fleet Air Arm Museum.
April 1994

Photographs.
All photographs unless otherwise captioned are from the Fleet Air Arm Museum Library from where copies can be obtained.

Type setting by
Maurice Biggs.

Printed by
Remous Ltd.
Milborne Port, Sherborne,
Dorset. DT9 5EP

ISBN No.
0 9513139 3 2

Cover photographs
Front ARK ROYAL 1978
Back INVINCIBLE 1980

CONTENTS

Section 1.

The Beginnings Pre 1914.

1. Men, Machines and Ideas........ 3

Section 2.

World War 1.

1. Development and operations. 8

Section 3.

1918-1939. The Difficult years.

1. Dual Control........ 18
2. Strategy and Tactics. 20
3. Ships and Aircraft........ 22

Section 4.

World War 2.

1. Pre War Carriers. 28
2. Trade Protection Carriers........ 30
3. Fleet Armoured Carriers........ 34

Section 5.

The next 35 Years.

1. Peace, Politics, Economics and Technology. 41
2. War Worn Carriers........ 44
3. Colossus Class Carriers........ 45
4. Centaur, Albion and Bulwark........ 47
5. Hermes. 49
6. Fleet Carriers........ 50

Section 6.

Vertical Take Off and Landing.

1. Policy and Politics. 53
2. Helicopter Carriers........ 54
3. Harrier Carriers. 56

Appendices.

List and Index of British Carriers........ 58

Index of Aircraft, Ships and Abbreviations........ 59

General Index........ 60

The Beginning. Pre 1914.

Men, Machines and Ideas.

It all began that day in December 1903 when the Wright Brothers made the first flight in an airplane at Kitty Hawk. The use of the air was entering the military equation. Other nations were developing airships, particularly in Germany. By 1908 the Board of Admiralty was interested in operating airships which had the advantage over airplanes that they could carry more people and more equipment such as wireless and bombs. They could also stay in the air longer. Airships were usually fitted with more than one engine which provided greater safety in the event of an engine failure. At that time airplanes could carry little more than the pilot. There was also concern that in the event of a war German airships might drop bombs on the British mainland and Royal Navy ships.

The first definite step was taken by the Admiralty in July 1908 when the Director of Naval Ordnance Captain R.S.Bacon DSO RN reported to the First Sea Lord, Admiral Sir John Fisher. His proposals included the suggestions that the War Office be approached concerning airship design, a Naval Assistant post should be created and a rigid type of airship should be constructed for the Navy. These proposals were considered by the Board of Admiralty and then submitted to the Committee of Imperial Defence. The Committee had been considering the effect of aircraft and airships on the defence of the country and had decided that the only way to assess this new weapon was to build and evaluate both aircraft and airships. The Committee asked that the sum of £35,000 should be included in the Naval Estimates for 1909/10 for the building of a rigid airship and a sum of £10,000 be included for the purchase of non-rigid airships and balloons.

The order for the rigid airship was placed with Vickers Sons & Maxim in May 1909. Captain Murray Sueter RN was appointed "Inspecting Captain of Aircraft" to oversee the construction of "No.1 Rigid Naval Airship" popularly known as "The Mayfly". Considering what happened the choice of the name was rather prophetic. The specification included very heavy items especially the two crew gondolas that were to be made of mahogany and able to survive impact with the water. While under construction it was obvious that the lifting power envisaged was not sufficient for the airship due to the heavy weight. The construction was therefore lightened as much as possible during the building. The first outing of the Mayfly was in May 1911 to the mooring mast outside the hangar where it withstood a wind gusting up to 40 mph for three days. Unfortunately when being returned to the hangar for preparations for the first flight the airship broke its back and was reduced to a total wreck. The Admiralty abandoned airship construction in January 1912.

It was in April 1909 that the Government appointed "The Advisory Committee for Aeronautics" to consider the foundation of the future Naval Air Service. One of the decisions the Committee made was to allow the National Physical Laboratory to open a new department for the investigation of aeronautics.

Eastchurch 1911. A Short Pusher Biplane Type S.27 Aircraft No. S.32

Meanwhile in America late in 1911 the US Navy had constructed a wooden platform 83ft x 24ft on the bows of the cruiser BIRMINGHAM. A Curtiss seaplane powered by a 50hp engine and piloted by Eugene Ely, a civilian, took off from the platform. Although the aircraft touched the water it eventually climbed away and landed at the Norfolk Naval base. The trial obviously impressed the US Navy as they sanctioned the construction of a landing on platform 119ft x 31½ft over the rear turret and stern of the cruiser PENNSYLVANIA. On 18 January 1912 Eugene Ely took off from land and landed on PENNSYLVANIA which was moored at the time. The landing distance was 30ft. The next day he took off from the same platform and landed at the airfield near San Francisco. The method used to stop the aircraft on the deck was by transverse wires with sandbags at the ends. The use of transverse wires was not to come into general use for nearly another 20 years.

In 1911 the Royal Aero Club informed the Admiralty that one of its members was prepared to lend two of his aircraft for the training of naval pilots. The member Mr F. McClean had already purchased an area of land for an aerodrome at Eastchurch in the Isle of Sheppey. The Admiralty, not being averse to receiving training without cost, called for volunteers and out of the 200 applicants four were selected. These officers all completed the course and gained their Royal Aero Club Aviator's certificates. The aircraft were later purchased by the Admiralty, and the airfield also became one of the naval shore stations.

Commander Oliver Schwann RN became interested in the possibility of an aircraft flying from water. To this end he purchased an Avro Type D for £700 and completed experiments with various types of floats. This was a completely private venture. In November 1911 Commander Oliver Schwann became the first English naval officer to take off from salt water but this was only for a short distance before the aircraft crashed. Early the next year the aircraft having been repaired it was successfully taken-off and landed by a Mr. S. V. Sippe and later by Commander Oliver Schwann who had by this time obtained his flying licence.(Note: Commander Schwann was later for a variety of reasons to change the spelling of his name to Swann)

During the year another of the early naval qualified pilots Lieutenant A.M. Longmore and the aircraft designer Mr Oswald Short had been conducting trials to fit aircraft with various types of floats and flotation bags.

Avro Type D owned by Commander Schwann being taxied by S.V.Sippe.

S.V.Sippe taking off from the water at Barrow-in-Furness.

The objective of the trials with flotation bags was to prevent total loss of an aircraft if it were forced to land in the sea. It was not intended that they would allow the aircraft to take off from the water. Longmore made a successful landing with an aircraft fitted with flotation bags on the Medway.

The next step in reasoning was obvious: could aircraft take off from, and land on, a ship at sea or would it be better to take off from the ship and land on the sea for recovery? Lieutenant C.R. Samson, another of the first pilots to qualify, convinced the Admiralty that an attempt should be made to see if an aircraft could take off from a ship. AFRICA was modified with a short deck built over the bows and fitted with parallel tracks in which the aircraft wheels could run. The track sloped down towards the bows so that gravity could help with the acceleration of the aircraft. In December 1911 he made a successful take off in a Short S.38 'pusher' biplane with the ship at anchor in Sheerness harbour. The aircraft was fitted with flotation bags along the sides of the wheel skids and was landed on the sea. Samson became the first Englishman to fly from a ship. After this flight the Admiralty sanctioned the construction of small take off areas on the foredeck of HIBERNIA and LONDON. During the Naval Review at Weymouth in May 1912 Lieutenant Samson made a successful take off from HIBERNIA in a Short S.38 biplane while the ship was steaming at 10kts. He later repeated the performance from LONDON steaming at 12kts.

Due to the loss of "The Mayfly" the Admiralty decided in January 1912 to close down airship construction and the special branch was disbanded. This decision was later to be reversed but the progress and development of the airship and balloons will not be considered in this book.

A number of problems were hampering aircraft development. Engine development had been slow, problems being experienced with increasing the engine power without a corresponding increase in weight. Due to the relatively low power of the engines the aircraft structure had to be fairly light. The storage of the aircraft on ships at sea where they were exposed to wind and waves caused many breakages of the light structures, the more so as the aircraft were not at this time able to have the wings folded and had to be kept in the normal rigged position. The introduction of floats and buoyancy bags added to the drag of the aircraft and the already low performance was further reduced.

Experiments had been commenced with wireless equipped aircraft. The range of the signal was not great due to the limitations on weight but a start on communications had been made. Various trials with armament and the dropping of bombs had been completed at Eastchurch.

On April 25 1912 the Committee of Imperial Defence received and approved a report concerning the organisation of the aeronautical services. This report stated that there should be a single aeronautical service under the title of "The Royal Flying Corps", which

HIBERNIA
Naval Review 1912 in Weymouth Bay
Short type S.38 being lifted on board after flight.

A Short Pusher S.38 mounted on the flying off ramp over the forward turret of HIBERNIA.

Short S.38 in position at the start of the flying off ramp on HIBERNIA. The two channels for the wheels clearly visible.

Lieutenant Samson taking off from HIBERNIA. underway off Weymouth in May 1912.

would be divided into Military and Naval Wings. All training would be completed at a central flying school that would be paid for jointly by the War Office and the Admiralty. Another suggestion in the report was that a consultative committee should be set up to be known as "The Air Committee". Once constituted this committee was soon aware that the requirements of the two Wings were different but the overall plan was that both organisations should provide a reserve of pilots for the other. This would mean that in the event of a naval war the whole of the Flying Corps would be available to the Naval Wing and in the event of a land battle all would be available to the Military Wing.

The official name of the new naval organisation was "Royal Flying Corps, Naval Wing". It would appear that this name did not find favour and was soon changed by common usage and then officially to "The Royal Naval Air Service". This meant that the words "Military Wing" now had no relevance and the military body became known as the "Royal Flying Corps".

November 1912 saw the formation at the Admiralty of the 'Air Department' under the direction of Captain Sueter. Shortly before this department was formed the principal duties of naval aircraft had been detailed. These were:

1 Distance reconnaissance work with the fleet at sea.

2. Reconnaissance work off the enemy's coasts, working from detached cruisers, or special aeroplane ships.

3. Assisting destroyers to detect and destroy submarines.

4. Detecting mine layers at work or mines that had already been laid.

5. Locating hostile craft in waters which have to be kept clear for war and merchant vessels.

6. Assisting submarines in their lookout for vessels to attack.

7. Screening the Fleet and harbours from observation by hostile aircraft, by attacking the latter.

8. Preventing attacks on dockyards, magazines, oil storage tanks by hostile aircraft.

The listing of these proposed duties goes some way in explaining why the Navy had such an interest in aerodromes and land based aircraft and seaplanes (see duties 7 and 8) and was not concentrating solely on aircraft carried on ships. These duties are not all that different from those of WW2.

The Admiralty was now more interested in the idea of ships carrying aircraft partly due to the airship developments in Germany and their possible use as an offensive force. The Admiralty had still to be convinced with further trials and not too much expenditure. To this end, and in accordance with a White Paper presented to the Committee of Imperial Defence in 1912, the 12 years old light cruiser HERMES was detailed for further trials under conditions that might be expected in wartime.

HERMES was commissioned for special duties as the parent ship of the Naval Wing of the Royal Flying Corps. A wooden take-off trackway was built on the forecastle above the forward 6in turret, additional stowage for three aircraft was made and derricks for the lifting of aircraft were fitted. The trials during the 1913 Naval Manoeuvres consisted of some flights being made with the aircraft lowered initially into the sea for take off and recovered after landing by the derrick, while others took off from the deck and landed on the sea for recovery. The aircraft used for the trials was a Short S.64 (No. 81) and equipped with an early W/T (Rouzet transmitter range 10 miles). The aircraft was fitted with a 160hp Gnome engine and also wings that could be folded. This first wing folding system was developed by Short Brothers. This type of modification classified the aircraft as a "Folder". The second aircraft was a Borel seaplane No. 48 with a 80hp Gnome engine. The first take-off by the Borel in heavy seas resulted in it being damaged beyond repair. The Short 64 was also damaged by heavy seas but was repaired. The Borel was replaced by a French built Caudron G.lll amphibian No.55 fitted with a 80hp Gnome. This aircraft was successfully launched from the bow platform while the ship steamed at 10kts. In all some 30 flights were made during these trials which showed that it was possible to operate

Sopwith Schneider No. 3734 taxying.

Borel being serviced by Naval personnel.

Short Folder No.119.

aeroplanes at sea and that the communication by radio was possible and effective. The Short S.64 also demonstrated the value of folding wings, as these aircraft required less storage space, were easier to handle and to protect from the elements. This feature became a standard requirement for ship based naval aircraft.

Towards the end of 1913 the Admiralty made the decision that the time had come to have a ship for exclusive use as an aircraft carrier. The First Lord of the Admiralty Winston Churchill announced that it had been decided to procure a special vessel at a cost of £81,000. The ship would carry seaplanes that could be lowered into the sea for take off and recovered after landing or could take off from a flying-off deck 130ft long. In ordering the vessel the major factors seem to have been firstly not to expend a great deal of money and secondly not to utilise building slips that were being used for the naval expansion. The Admiralty purchased a collier that was under construction. As the construction was not too far advanced it was possible to relocate the engine room aft and to provide a large stowage space for 10 aircraft in the hold 40ft long and 30ft wide amidships There were two steam cranes to lift the aircraft. Beneath the bridge there was a shelter where the aircraft's engine could be run for maintenance purposes. Also contained in the ship would be stowage for aircraft fuel, magazines for bombs and torpedoes and spare parts for the aircraft. The ship was named ARK ROYAL and launched in September 1914.

World War 1. 1914 to 1918

Development and Operations.

The new seaplane carrier ARK ROYAL could not be ready for use until January 1915, so the Navy had to look elsewhere when World War one broke out on the 4th August 1914. It immediately commandeered three cross channel passenger ships, ENGADINE, EMPRESS and RIVIERA, which could steam at 22 knots. Wooden platforms were built fore and aft with canvas screens as a hangar. These were replaced with permanent steel covered hangars with doors in 1915.

ENGADINE with a Short 184 ready to be lifted. The nose is pointing to the hangar.

The Germans had built a considerable number of airships which they used to attack shipping in the Channel and North Sea, as well as against England itself. The first ever Carrier Task Force was sent to attack the German airship sheds at Cuxhaven at the mouth of the river Elbe in Heligoland Bay. ENGADINE, EMPRESS and RIVIERA carried nine seaplanes under the command of Squadron Commander L'Estrange Malone and were accompanied by two cruisers, ten destroyers and twelve submarines. Each aircraft carried three 20 lb bombs and no guns except for the pilot's revolver. He was also expected to carry tools and spare plugs etc. in case the engine gave trouble, when he would land, fix it and take off again.

The Fleet was off Heligoland on Christmas morning 1914 and the aircraft were hoisted out. Two would not start and the other seven were airborne by 0715.

The Fleet was attacked by two Zeppelins and three seaplanes and eleven bombs were dropped on EMPRESS but there were no hits. Freezing fog over the coast caused difficulties for the aircraft none of which found the target airship sheds but between them they dropped ten bombs on a cruiser, a submarine, a shore battery and seaplane sheds. Not much damage was done but it did cause the Germans to move some ships into the Baltic. Of the seven seaplanes only two flew back to the fleet. Two came down for engine repairs, one returning to a destroyer which towed it back to the carrier, whilst the other pilot had to sink his near a Dutch trawler and return home via Holland. Three pilots landed near a submarine which rescued them but the aircraft were lost. In his report Squadron Commander Malone stressed the need for reliable aircraft armed with a torpedo or a gun.

This modest raid by modern standards was to lead in World War 2 to such successful carrier aircraft attacks as the Royal Navy at Taranto and the Japanese at Pearl Harbor where the Italian and United States battleship fleets were sunk by bombs and torpedoes.

Shipborne aircraft have another important role as "The Eyes of the Fleet". No modern fleet can operate without them but in 1916 the Navy had not yet come to rely on its aircraft. There was also the problem that communications were difficult. Nevertheless aircraft were present at the Battle of Jutland. It was 1740 on the 30th May 1916 when the British Grand Fleet was ordered to raise steam and put to sea to meet the German Fleet. Admiral Beatty's Battle Cruiser Fleet sailed from the Firth of Forth at 2300 and with it went ENGADINE, the first aircraft carrier to take part in a fleet action. A second carrier CAMPANIA followed two hours later as it was late in receiving the order to sail. CAMPANIA was a converted former Cunard liner with a bow platform.It carried seven single seat fighters which could have provided protection from airships and also three Short 184 aircraft fitted with wireless which could be used for reconnaissance. Admiral Jellicoe ordered CAMPANIA to return to harbour as there was the danger of submarine attack. Possibly the importance of aerial attack and defence had still to be appreciated.

ENGADINE was positioned between the 1st Light Cruiser Squadron to port and the 2nd to starboard. The two Battle Cruiser Squadrons were ten miles away on its port quarter and the 5th Battle Squadron containing four QUEEN ELIZABETH class fast battleships five miles beyond them. It was 1420 when the cruiser GALATEA reported sighting two enemy cruisers and the Battle of Jutland had begun. It soon became apparent that there were more enemy ships and the Admiral signalled ENGADINE to send up an aeroplane to scout to the northeast. Twenty minutes later Short 184 No. 8359 was airborne with Flight Lieutenant Rutland as pilot and Assistant Paymaster Trewin as observer. A second reconnaissance plane and a single seat Short were made ready in case they were needed.

Low cloud kept the aircraft below 1000 feet and visibility varied between nil and four miles. Trewin sighted the enemy through the clouds and sent three reports in the next fifteen minutes, the most important being the enemy's change of course from northwest to south. Unfortunately a petrol pipe broke and Rutland had to land near ENGADINE. He was able to repair the pipe with some rubber tubing which formed part of the pilot's repair kit but was not allowed to take off again and the aircraft was hoisted on board. No further flights were ordered by the Admiral from ENGADINE which had dropped several miles astern of the fleet which was now steaming south at twenty five knots.

Aircraft 8359 survived the war and was given to the Imperial War Museum in London where it was unfortunately damaged by enemy bombing during World War 2. The remains of the fuselage with the two cockpits and engine are now in the Fleet Air Arm Museum at Royal Naval Air Station Yeovilton, not far from Westlands at Yeovil where it was built.

CAMPANIA which had not been allowed to take part in the Battle of Jutland was an unusual looking aircraft carrier. The 20,750 ton ship had been a record breaking trans-Atlantic liner with a speed of 21 knots for twenty years and in 1914 was sold for scrap as being worn out. The RNAS needed seaplane carriers but all available ships had already been taken for other uses so CAMPANIA was reluctantly bought from the breakers in 1914. A large wooden flying-off deck was fitted over the bow to be used for the launching of seaplanes on wheeled trolleys whilst the ship was under way. The more usual method was to hoist the seaplanes over the side with the ship stopped and it would then take off from the water, providing it was not too rough. CAMPANIA was commissioned on 17th April 1915 under Wing Captain Oliver Swann and joined the Grand Fleet on 11th June when her aircraft became the first ever to provide air reconnaissance for a fleet at sea. On 8th August 1915 Flight Lieutenant W.Welsh flew a Sopwith Schneider seaplane on a wheeled trolley off CAMPANIA's wooden deck. This was the first time this had been done since Charles Samson had flown off HERMES two years before.

The ship's flight deck was later increased in length by replacing the forefunnel with two small ones on either side of the flight deck which was extended between them. Beneath the deck was a hangar for ten seaplanes. Owing to its age the ship was relegated to a training role and during a gale on 5th November 1918 in the Firth of Forth, she dragged her anchors and collided with the battleship ROYAL OAK and then the battlecruiser GLORIOUS and sank.

CAMPANIA was the second aircraft carrier to have a hangar beneath the flight deck. This was between the two fore funnels and could hold six Fairey seaplanes in two rows, three abreast. The seaplane's floats were secured to trolleys and the trolleys secured to the deck. The plane in the middle of the forward row had to be lifted out first and the others then moved to that position for lifting out in turn. Each plane was rested on the deck beside the hangar for its wings to be spread.

CAMPANIA at anchor with a Short 184 taking off..

When the ship was at anchor the seaplane was lowered over the side by derrick ready for flying off. Returning to the ship at anchor, the aircraft landed on the sea and came along-side the ship. The observer stood on a float to catch a line thrown to him by a man at the end of the boom, the line was secured and the engine stopped. The pilot then stood on the fuselage and hooked on to the derrick ready for hoisting inboard.

When the ship was under way the planes flew off from the flight deck. The seaplane was hoisted up from the hangar and lowered onto a four wheeled axle which was secured to the fuselage with a quick release wire. It was manhandled

CAMPANIA second conversion. The angle of the flying off deck is 5 degrees. The lift is visible at the top of the flying off deck. The two large crates are where the hangar will be.

CAMPANIA.
Fairey Campania with wings extended on the set of four jettisonable wheels, being placed in position for takeoff.

BEN-MY-CHREE.
Two aircraft visible in the rear hangar.

between the two funnels and the wings spread. The ship steamed into wind to get enough wind speed over the deck, the engine was run up to full speed and the quick release wire holding the plane was let go. When airborne the observer released the wheels which were picked up by the destroyer escort.

On return to the ship, the pilot would land ahead of the ship keeping head to wind and the ship would come up to the plane without stopping. The observer standing on the fuselage would catch the hook of the derrick, hook on the plane, the pilot stopped the engine and they were hoisted on board. This procedure undoubtedly needed a calm sea and a lot of practice.

The speed of launching and recovering of aircraft by ships at sea has always been of the greatest importance in operational conditions. When a ship is stopped it becomes an easy target for enemy submarines and aircraft. It also delays the other ships when sailing in company. When operating with a fleet the carrier is normally expected to detach itself with its escorts, fly off and recover its aircraft, and then catch up with the fleet and get back into position. Hence the need for carrier operations to be efficient and quick which the handling of seaplanes was not. The Navy needed aircraft with wheels which could take off and land on the carriers. With the ships available in World War 1 take off was possible but not landing on again.

The first seaplane carrier with a hangar and with other facilities for handling aircraft was ARK ROYAL which came into service in January 1915. The opening of the Dardanelles Campaign in February found her giving 'mobile' air support for the naval bombardment of the Turkish Outer Forts. Her seaplanes spotted for the ships although they had limitations for this work. Her mobility enabled her aircraft to be brought into use where the aircraft would not otherwise be available and helped considerably. At the end of May, however, German submarines appeared and sank two battleships and it was decided that ARK ROYAL was too slow to operate with her 10 knots maximum speed . She therefore remained at anchor in Kephalo Bay, Imbros, acting as a depot ship for all aircraft while her own aircraft continued to operate from the bay. In June the seaplane carrier BEN-MY-CHREE arrived in the area and with her speed of 24 knots was able to provide the mobility that ARK ROYAL lacked.

BEN-MY-CHREE was the fastest packet to the Isle of Man and had been requisitioned for naval service. Like the other ferries she was used as a seaplane carrier but the stern hangar was more substantial. She carried four planes. Her main task was spotting for bombardments but the aircraft also carried out patrols over enemy territory.

The ship had brought with it torpedoes and on the 12th August Short No 842 piloted by Flight Commander Edmonds took off with a 14 inch torpedo and off Injeh Burnu near Gallipoli sighted a 8,000 ton steamer. He made a gliding approach to attack and dropped the torpedo at a height of about 15 feet and a range of 800 yards. The torpedo was seen to hit the ship which settled by the stern Five days later he torpedoed another ship which was gutted by fire. Another seaplane piloted by Flight Lieutenant Dacre was also airborne but had engine trouble so he had to land and then looked for a suitable target. He found a large tug in False Bay, taxied across the Narrows and released his torpedo which hit the tug and sank it. He retreated on the surface from rifle fire from the shore and eventually was able to take off and return to BEN-MY-CHREE.

These attacks were the first and only successful aerial torpedo attacks of World War 1 as the heavily laden Short seaplane could only take off in ideal conditions of a calm sea and a slight breeze. Nevertheless they affected the enemy's morale: perhaps more importantly they proved that torpedo attacks by aircraft could be successful. In World War 2 they were decisive.

In 1916 BEN-MY-CHREE with two converted ex German freighters carrying one or two seaplanes each, formed the East Indies and Egypt Seaplane Squadron, command of which was taken over in May by Commander Charles Samson, with an Army Officer Lieutenant J Wedgwood Benn as his observer. One of his first tasks was to improve the launching and recovery procedures which required the ship to be stopped for far too long in waters where German submarines operated.

ARK ROYAL. Sopwith 807 on the forward deck. Entrance to the hangar under the bridge can be seen, also the two steam cranes.

ARK ROYAL. A Short 166 being hoisted out by steam crane. The identification Union Jacks were used in the early stages of the war, later replaced by the normal roundels.

HMS ARK ROYAL. View from the bridge above the deck hangar. The storage hold under the deck can be seen, behind the two steam cranes are two Short 166 seaplanes. Photograph taken at Kephalo in 1915.

He used the ship to form a lee of calmer water for the seaplane to land on and the observer to hook on to the derrick so that with practice the ship was able to hoist out a seaplane and recover a second one within forty five seconds.

The aircraft were used in bombing raids on towns and airfields on the Palestine coast, the bombs being 20 and 65 lbs. In June BEN-MY-CHREE sailed through the Suez Canal and Red Sea to Aden which was threatened by Turkish troops. The intense heat meant that the water-cooled Short seaplanes could only fly early in the morning or in the late afternoon because of over heating. On the way Samson's aircraft made a reconnaissance of the Turkish positions and was able to present the senior naval and army officers in Aden with a detailed report and map of the Turkish positions. This emphasised the importance of aerial reconnaissance. The aircraft made bombing attacks on the enemy forces and on returning to the Mediterranean continued their support of the operations there. In January 1917 BEN-MY-CHREE entered the harbour at Castelorizo to put up flights in support of the French. The Turks opened fire on the ship and the port and the surrounding hills. The ship was hit, caught fire and had to be abandoned.

Seaplanes were carried on other ships and proved their usefulness. One instance was in finding the German raider KONIGSBERG which had caused havoc amongst allied shipping off the east coast of Africa and sunk a British light cruiser. The ship had taken refuge in the Rufiji Delta in German East Africa and proved difficult to locate. Flt Sub Lt H.D.Cutler flying a requisitioned Curtiss flying boat was able to find the enemy ship. KONIGSBERG was subsequently destroyed by naval gunfire directed by RNAS landplanes operating from Mafia Island off the mouth of the river delta. Earlier attempts using floatplanes had failed when the high prevailing temperatures had reduced performance so much that the aircraft were unable to carry an observer or a full fuel load.

In 1916 a hopper barge SLINGER (Navy was not devoid of a sense of humour) was converted to conduct trials on ship catapults. Nothing came of the trials as the aircraft then in use could take off from very short distances. However the idea of the catapult was not forgotten and came into service between the wars.

The conversion of another Isle of Man packet VIKING-renamed VINDEX- was completed in August 1915 with two hangars, one aft to carry four large and one small seaplane and another on the flying off deck forward for two fighter planes. The first successful flight from a carrier deck by a landplane was made from VINDEX by Flight Lieutenant H.F.Towler in a Bristol

Scout on 3 November 1915. On 29 July 1916 Flight Lieutenant C.T.Freeman made the first attack on a German airship by an aeroplane which had taken off from a ship. He flew a Bristol Scout from VINDEX and dropped Rankin darts on L.17 which broke away and later attacked East Anglia. The Rankin darts weighed 1.lb. and contained explosive and black powder which were dropped onto the airship to set fire to the hydrogen gas bags.

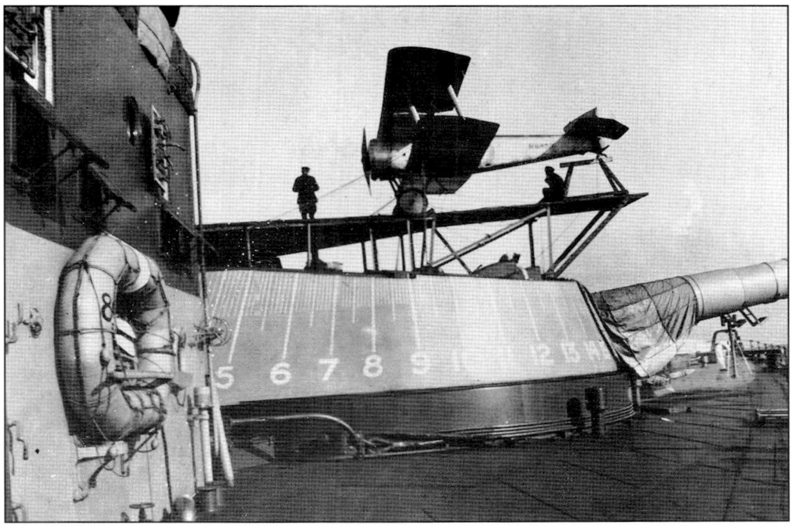
Sopwith Pup on a platform mounted on a gun turret.

Other packets MANXMAN, NAIRANA and PEGASUS were converted in the same way. The MANXMAN proved slower than expected and usually could not fly off single engine float planes from the front deck. It was apparent that float equipped aircraft did not have the performance to be able to intercept the German airships, a matter which concerned the Admiralty greatly and showed the need for carriers that could operate wheeled aircraft.

Trials with Sopwith Pup wheeled fighters were an immediate success, take off distances being in the region of 20 feet given a reasonable wind over the deck. This success led to the carrying of wheeled fighter and reconnaissance aircraft on normal warships. Initially the short take off platform was fixed to the warship Launching the aircraft involved the ship leaving the formation and steaming into wind. This was unacceptable and later the platform was mounted on one of the gun turrets which could then be rotated into wind. The aircraft were fitted with wheels and flotation bags, but considered expendable if recovery meant the carrier leaving the formation. By 1918 many battleships and cruisers were fitted with one or two aircraft, either fighter or reconnaissance aircraft.

Sopwith 1½ Strutter taking off from gun platform on RENOWN 1917.

Another method of taking fighter aircraft with the Grand Fleet was the use of towed lighters. These had first been used to take reconnaissance flying boats into an area to increase their operational range. On 31st July 1918 a successful take off was made by Lieutenant S.D.Culley in a Camel N6812 from a lighter being towed at a speed of 30 knots. This method was to prove its worth as on the 10th August Lieutenant Culley took off from a lighter being towed at 30 knots by REDOUBT to intercept a Zeppelin L53. After climbing to 18,000 feet he attacked the airship from below and it caught fire and was destroyed. The higher performance of the wheeled aircraft with the limited engine power then available was proved to be essential. All these early experiments were giving pointers to what would eventually be required for the aircraft carrier. It was now becoming clear that the requirement was for wheeled aircraft to be able to take off from and land on while the ship was proceeding at speed with the fleet.

Sopwith 1½ Strutter taking off.

Apart from CAMPANIA all the aircraft carriers were quite small and for the most part operated only seaplanes. There was a need for larger ships which could operate wheeled planes from their flight decks. Commander Hugh Williamson, a pilot and submariner, had put forward ideas for using aircraft against submarines and flying from ships, as long ago as 1912. In 1915 he was appointed to the Air Department and developed his concept of the aircraft carrier, reasoning that the main necessity for flying from a deck was a clear flow of air over it. His idea was to move the ship's bridge, funnel and mast, the so called "Island", to the starboard side leaving a clear deck from stem to stern and the full width of the ship.

Commander Gerrard Holmes, a reserve officer and naval architect, suggested a clear deck with no superstructure at all.

Admiral Jellicoe the Commander in Chief of the Grand Fleet had also urged the Admiralty to build a better carrier and it was decided in August 1916 to buy a partly built Italian passenger ship of 15,750 tons and a speed of 19 knots. This was named ARGUS but would not be ready before September 1918. It was therefore decided in March 1917 to take over FURIOUS, a light battlecruiser of 19,513 tons, launched in August 1916 and nearing completion. This ship had the added advantage of a speed of 31 knots.

Sopwith Camel handling crew and Samson on a towed lighter

FURIOUS had an 18 inch gun fore and aft. The forward gun was replaced with a large hangar to take ten aircraft and a flight deck was built over it for flying off wheeled aircraft. This deck was 228 feet long and 50 feet wide. The central superstructure and the aft gun remained. She was commissioned on 26th June 1917 and joined the Grand Fleet with three Short 184 seaplanes and five Sopwith Pup landplanes. The Pups would fly off the flight deck but on return land in the water, kept afloat by airbags until hoisted back on board. Squadron Commander E.H.Dunning was confident that he could land a Pup on the flight deck and this he did on 2nd August 1917, side slipping around the bridge superstructure. This was the first ever landing of an aircraft on a ship underway. Unfortunately Dunning was killed on 7th August making his third attempt at landing. Further attempts were forbidden.

Sopwith Camel on a lighter being towed at speed by a destroyer

It was then decided to give FURIOUS a flying on deck aft. Between November 1917 and March 1918 the aft gun and mainmast were replaced with an aircraft hangar and a deck on top 284 feet long and 70 feet wide, together with lifts from both fore and aft hangars to the deck above. The two decks were connected on both sides to allow aircraft to move from one deck to the other. When completed the ship could carry sixteen wheeled aircraft. Arrester wires were stretched fore and aft at nine inches above the deck, across which ropes were laid attached to sandbags at each end. At the forward end of the arrester wires there was another ramp sloping upwards.

First succesful flight test of a Sopwith Camel at the end of July 1918.
Pilot Flying Officer Culley from Fighter Flight Great Yarmouth.

The Sopwith Pups were fitted with skids and also hooks to take up the transverse arrester wires. In addition a rope barrier was erected forward of the wires to prevent an aircraft which failed to hook on from crashing into the central superstructure which still remained. Attempts to land on the new deck aft proved almost impossible mainly due to air turbulence caused by the superstructure of bridge and funnel in the middle of the ship between the two decks, as well as the hot gases discharging from the funnel. The funnel and bridge would have to be moved to one side and successful changes were made after the war ended.

ARGUS with aircraft ready to take off.

Sopwith Pup fitted with skids on FURIOUS. Visible are the V shaped hooks on the undercarriage which engage on the wires. The rope with sandbags on the end that was at right angles to the arrester wires can be seen round the hooks.

A Sopwith 1½ Strutter in the centre of the arrester wires. The height of the wires above the deck is illustrated by the position of the wire in reference to the handling crews legs. The height did not make rapid movement across the deck possible. Just in front of the handling crew can be seen matting which was intended to halt the aircraft. Taken on FURIOUS 1.10.1918

This did not prevent FURIOUS from carrying out the final major naval air operation of the war. On 19th June 1918 the ship was attacked by two German seaplanes in the North sea. Two Camels from her complement of sixteen aircraft were launched and Lieutenant Grahame Heath shot down one of the German planes to record the first such victory by a carrier based aircraft.

On 19th July 1918 FURIOUS was at sea with the 1st Light Cruiser Squadron, and destroyers, supported by the 1st Division of the Battle Fleet and the 7th Light Cruiser Squadron, to launch an aircraft attack on the airship base at Tondern in Denmark. Seven Camel aircraft took off but one had to return with engine trouble before reaching the target. The other six located the target and between them dropped twelve 50lb bombs. The largest shed along with two airships inside it, were set alight and destroyed. Another shed was badly damaged and a gas tanker was hit. Only one aircraft returned safely and another pilot came down near an escort after three hours and fifteen minutes in the air. One pilot was lost and the other three landed in Denmark.

FURIOUS after the first conversion still retaining the single 18in gun aft. Sopwith Pup flying towards the flying off deck.

The newly built carrier ARGUS was the world's first ever flush deck carrier. The intention had been initially for ARGUS to have a superstructure split into two halves one on each side of the ship with a flight deck running between the two and a bridge connecting the two islands. However because of the difficulties experienced with disturbed airflow on FURIOUS the design of ARGUS was to be changed to a complete flush deck. Her hangar below the deck could hold twenty torpedo carrying Sopwith Cuckoos or eighteen seaplanes. The charthouse in the middle of the deck could be lowered when flying was in progress. There were two lifts from hangar to deck. The funnels ran below the flight deck to discharge at the stern. Arrester wires were fitted and the aircraft had hooks to catch them. ARGUS was completed in September 1918 and the trials for flying on and off the ship were entirely successful. The world's first shipborne torpedo squadron, equipped with the world's first purpose designed torpedo bomber, the Sopwith Cuckoo, was embarked on ARGUS on 19th October 1918, too late to take part in hostilities. The Sopwith Cuckoo wheeled aircraft was developed from the B.1. land bomber, carried an 18in torpedo and had a crude sighting device for dropping the torpedo. It was specially designed for carrier operation and carried no other armament apart from the torpedo.

Aircraft carriers in the Royal Navy had developed from ad hoc seaplane carriers to a purpose built vessel able to fly off and land on the most advanced wheeled aircraft which were armed with torpedoes capable of sinking major ships. No other navy had either the ships or the experience to operate aircraft carriers.

FURIOUS after the second conversion showing the connections between the two flying decks. Behind the wind screens on the flying off deck there is a Sopwith 1½ Strutter. The lift is in the down position. On the flying on deck there is a Submarine Scout Type 7 Airship. The barrier to protect aircraft from hitting the superstructure is still rigged.

Sopwith 1½ Strutter making a trial landing. Aircraft has just passed over the forward ramp and is about to drop into the arrester wire well.

Sopwith Camels on the flying off deck of FURIOUS protected by wind barriers.

Sopwith Cuckoo dropping torpedo.

1918-1939. The Difficult Years.

Dual Control.

The Royal Naval Air Service (RNAS) had become part of the newly created Royal Air Force (RAF) on 1st April 1918 when it combined with the Royal Flying Corps (RFC) and both Army and Navy lost control of their air services. During the war both services had developed their air services in parallel, with the inevitable duplication of support and other services. Both operated similar bomber and fighter squadrons in action against the German enemy. Strategic bombing had been pioneered by the RNAS. There had been conflicts over the supply of aircraft in 1916: the RFC used those built by the Royal Aircraft Factory whilst the RNAS preferred private makers which were better and the RFC naturally wanted the better ones also. A committee appointed to sort the matter out was unable to agree. An Air Board was then set up under Lord Curzon to promote better co-operation between the two services and to formulate policy for the future of the Air Service as a whole. There were Service representatives on the Board but they had no part in preparing Lord Curzon's report five months later. This stated that the RNAS when Winston Churchill was First Lord of the Admiralty, had unfair advantages over the Army, despite which it had not been effective in using these resources, whilst the Army's RFC had been bearing the brunt on the Western Front. Also the RNAS had not prevented the attacks by German airships on the British mainland. "A single policy, co-ordination of airforces and the management of the RNAS by airmen rather than seamen would have produced better results". This report sowed the seeds of amalgamation.

In 1917, following more German air raids on London, another committee was set up under Lieutenant General Smuts the South African and former Boer enemy. The Air Board newly set up earlier in 1917 asked that it should become a permanent Ministry with a War staff. Smuts found in favour of a single unified Air Service and the Air Force (Constitutional) Bill was approved by the House of Commons on 8th November 1917, to take effect on 1st April 1918.

The Navy was perhaps partly responsible because the possibilities of air power for the navy had not been fully appreciated or developed despite the success of the seaplane carriers like BEN-MY-CHREE. A proper aircraft carrier had yet to be produced and apart from the airmen themselves, the big guns and battleships were still regarded as the primary weapon for both the present and future. Even in 1945 when Japan surrendered it was a battleship which took pride of place when the British Pacific Fleet which was really a Carrier Task Force, entered Tokyo Bay.

During World War 1 the RNAS had expanded to 55,000 officers and men which was way beyond what could possibly be retained in peacetime and all but 1300 were wartime only. Aviation for officers was just another specialisation and promotion depended on general naval experience which most aviators lacked. As a consequence most of them transferred to the new RAF where many, including Samson and Longmore who had been two of the original four who had become pilots, achieved high rank. This left the Navy short of officers with experience and knowledge of aviation, particularly in senior ranks in the years leading up to and during World War 2.

The economies of peace added to demobilisation brought drastic reductions in personnel in all three services; both the Army and the Navy wanted to get back control of their flying services whilst the RAF under Trenchard was striving to survive intact. The Navy was led by Admiral Beatty and there were continuing discussions as to how the Navy's flying needs would be met, particularly the arrangements for fliers themselves and what titles and uniforms they would wear. Instead of merely seeking control of the FAA which served the Navy, the Admiralty, probably unwisely, joined forces with the War Office in arguing for the abolition of the RAF and a return to the old separate army and naval air services. The Geddes Committee of National Expenditure, which eventually recommended substantial cuts in the armed forces, the so called "Geddes Axe", received arguments from the Army and Navy that separate services run by them would be more economical but Trenchard persuaded the Committee to the contrary view. In December 1921 Geddes reported in favour of keeping the Air Force but at the same time recommended bigger cuts in the Air Estimates than for the other services.

Hawker Nimrod. 800 Squadron.

Beatty and the Navy continued to press for control of the FAA but had lost the sympathy of the politicians like Churchill who had supported them. Following the collapse of the coalition government and the election of the Conservatives under Bonar Law, a committee was set up in 1923 under Lord Salisbury to consider the place of air power in the national defence. This had a sub committee under Lord Balfour to look at the problems of the FAA. The other members were Lords Weir and Peel and Sir Maurice Hankey the Secretary. Balfour who had been First Lord of the Admiralty, was sympathetic to the naval view whilst Weir was a former Air Minister and favoured the Air Force. Neither could be persuaded to change his view so Hankey suggested a visit to Portsmouth to see the aircraft carriers ARGUS and EAGLE. Balfour who was elderly and unwell could not go but the others were impressed by the good relations which they found existed in the ships. As a result Balfour was persuaded to modify his wish for complete transfer of the FAA to the Navy.

The Committee made several concessions to the Navy so that the Admiralty would pay for the FAA: all observers would be naval personnel and seventy percent of the pilots would be naval but attached to the RAF though continuing to wear naval uniform. The Admiralty continued to object but the Government accepted the Balfour committee's decision though it was to be regarded as experimental. A year later Lord Haldane was asked to mediate and met Trenchard and Admiral Keyes which resulted in the Trenchard-Keyes agreement and established the Dual Control system under which the Admiralty and the Air Ministry shared responsibility for the FAA for the next 14 years.

Despite continued grumbling at Admiralty Board level, naval and air force personnel got on well in happy ships. There were difficulties, however, in getting enough naval officers to volunteer as pilots, mainly because they were worried about future promotion prospects. They also had to have commissions in the Air Force as well as the Navy which could cause problems. The Navy also had difficulties in building up sufficient reserve numbers. In any event these were going to be quite inadequate as the loss of pilots in the event of war was expected to be quite low apart from some major fleet action. The Norwegian campaign in 1940 showed this to be a fallacy.

In 1934 the Navy wished to train rating pilots to help meet the shortage of officer pilots covered by the Balfour decision but the Air Ministry prevaricated as it had done several years earlier, finally agreeing to train a few. The Danby Fleet Air Arm Committee was set up in October 1934 to look at the working and organisation of the FAA. The members were mainly experienced naval aviators and the Chairman was an Admiral who had commanded the aircraft carrier FURIOUS. It concluded that the difficulties including those of personnel were due to the Dual Control policy arrangements. In May 1935 the Board of Admiralty decided to try to get full control of the FAA. Sir Maurice Hankey was again involved in attempting mediation but the First Sea Lord Admiral Sir Ernle Chatfield made it clear that the Navy wanted full control as experience had shown this to be necessary and mediation was not possible.

In April 1936 the First Sea Lord wrote to Sir Thomas Inskip the Minister for the Co-ordination of Defence drawing his attention to the problem, particularly the shortage of pilots and observers and inadequate reserves. This did not please the Air Minister nor Lord Weir of the Balfour Committee and still a Government adviser on air matters. In November Inskip merely recommended minor changes even though he accepted the situation was unsatisfactory and the absence of common ground between the services was disquieting. He suggested that there might be a need for a further enquiry. This satisfied neither side. It became accepted that another enquiry was

Avro Bison Mk.II. 423 Flight ARGUS. N9848

needed and that two other Ministers should assist Inskip but as usual there was haggling over the terms which dragged on for months. Lord Weir threatened to resign if an enquiry were held and Chatfield threaten to resign as First Sea Lord if an early decision was not made. The matter was raised in the House of Commons and in the press with Churchill, Trenchard, Keyes and others all joining in. At the end of June 1937 it was agreed that Inskip should act alone. He reported on 21st July 1937 and recommended that the Admiralty should become fully responsible for the FAA but Coastal Command should remain with the RAF. Despite strong objections from the Air Ministry the change was accepted by the government and came into effect on 24th May 1939. It was also agreed that the RAF would lend the Navy maintenance personnel until it could train its own. The Navy took over a number of air stations which were necessary to provide facilities for training and for disembarked squadrons of aircraft and personnel.

Having regained full control of the FAA the Admiralty now had to prepare for war which was likely to start very soon, in particular it had to recruit and train pilots and other aircrew as well as creating an entirely new maintenance organisation and training the necessary mechanics and other support staff.

1918-1939. The Difficult Years.

Strategy and Tactics.

With the transfer of the RNAS to the RAF the Navy had lost most of its experienced and senior air officers as well as the Air Staff. One who stayed was Commander Bell Davies who had won a VC for rescuing another pilot behind enemy lines. He became the head of the newly formed Naval Air Section of the Naval Staff but this embryo department took many years to become an autonomous department. Its duties were to assist the Assistant Chief of Naval Staff (ACNS) and it was concerned with the practical ways and means rather than the long term tactical or strategic needs. This was not the dynamic leadership found in the air service of the United States Navy which retained full control. The air service was represented on the Admiralty Board by ACNS who, like the rest of the Board, was a gunner though usually an enthusiast for Air Power.

Throughout the 1920s there was general economic retrenchment and disarmament. The naval staff was reduced and senior officers had other problems and no time to consider the purpose of air power in the fleet. No one wished to create an Air Staff which might compete with and upset the Air Ministry but rather to integrate with the Navy so responsibility for policy was diffused and spread among many departments. This included the design and construction of aircraft which in any case was the responsibility of the Air Ministry.

Things were at a low ebb when in 1931 Rear Admiral R.G.H.Henderson was given the new post of Rear Admiral Aircraft Carriers. He was not an aviator but was an exponent of air power and had commanded FURIOUS. This move raised morale and also performance in the FAA. He later became Third Sea Lord and pressed for the Armoured Carrier Programme. His early death in 1939 was a great loss. His successor was Admiral Ramsey who became Fifth Sea Lord and Chief of the Naval Air Service. Between 1932 and 1934 things improved and there was the beginning of an expansion programme. The Naval Air Division was also starting to think about naval air tactics. The first of the post war flyers were also getting their staff appointments. They were gaining in technical expertise and one member, Captain Rawlings, was a friend of Richard Fairey and was largely responsible for the production of that legendary aircraft the Swordfish. There were difficulties with getting suitable radio equipment and bomb sights for moving targets from the Air Ministry which was more concerned with fixed land targets. Departments of Air Material and of Air Personnel were set up in January 1938 after the Inskip Award.

Blackburn Blackburn Mk.I.

Both the United States and Japan had long term plans for naval aviation but the spread of responsibility around several Admiralty departments meant that no one had suggested a plan for British naval air power. However a paper on aircraft in cruisers circulated by Captain Rawlings and NAD in January 1934 resulted in a diversity of views on the use of air power. As a consequence the various staff divisions together produced in March 1936 the first

EAGLE. A view from the rear cockit of a Swordfish which had just taken off.

part of a manual on Fleet Air Arm Tactics and Equipment, this part dealing with FAA functions in a fleet action.

This was to be followed by another dealing with trade protection. The Sea Lords were not fully in agreement with it and were concerned not to be telling the Fleet Commanders what to do so that it had to be modified before sending it out generally. It should be remembered that it took a long time in those days to get mail all around the world and it was a year before it had been discussed and the differing views received. No revised edition and no second volume on trade protection were ever issued. The clear possibility of war and the need for expansion prompted another committee under Rear Admiral Holland to produce the Fleet's Air Requirements in War. This report set out the number of ships and aircraft needed, their roles and functions and discussed their tactical employment both for the fleet and trade protection. At last firm guidance had been given.

Fairey IIIF. With propeller spinner removed.

The role of the FAA depended on the role of the Navy itself which was held by the Admiralty to be that of the Grand Fleet. It was generally accepted that in a war the Navy sooner or later would have to fight a major fleet action. This action would be fought by the big guns of the opposing fleets. The role of aircraft was to help find the enemy before he found us so as to obtain surprise if possible. Having found the enemy the aircraft would then assist the gunnery by spotting fall of shot and reporting this so that corrections could be made. If aircraft could damage and slow down the enemy this was an advantage. If the enemy were fleeing then crippling by aircraft was the only means of bringing him to battle. The aircraft therefore needed to be armed with torpedoes or bombs. The Navy considered dive bombing was the best method against moving ships but the Air Force and Bomber Command who were mainly dealing with land based targets concentrated on high level bombing. A similar difference of opinion existed in America between the Navy and Army Air Forces.

The Royal Navy had the first purpose designed torpedo carrying aircraft in 1918 when a Squadron of Sopwith Cuckoos was embarked in ARGUS and the tactics of use had been developed. They flew to the target in formation using cloud, the sun or heat haze to avoid visual detection and then usually attacked in formation together or in waves. The aircraft approached the target flying parallel to it, then in a shallow dive towards it and then steeply, levelling out at 100 feet or less dropping at around 1000 yards from the target. The aircraft then took action to avoid the gunfire and returned to the carrier, preferably in company with other aircraft.

The Navy practised this form of attack and tests were also carried out to find the effectiveness of bombing against the target ship CENTURIAN. This showed dive bombing to be much more effective in the number of hits than high level bombing. There was also consideration of the possibility of attacking a fleet in harbour and in 1936 the use of such an attack against the Italian fleet was thought to be an option during the Abyssinian crisis. Indeed it became a reality in November 1940 when the FAA destroyed the Italian fleet at Taranto with torpedoes.

Fighters were needed by the fleet to shoot down enemy reconnaissance planes preferably before they had sighted and reported on our ships, as well as protecting the spotting planes. Fighters had a shorter time in the air which made it more difficult to provide continuous patrols over the fleet so that the Navy advocated two seat long range fighters for escorting strike aircraft with an observer to navigate so they could find the carrier on return with less difficulty. There was an argument as to whether anti aircraft guns on ships were effective against attacking aircraft this being almost impossible to evaluate without shooting at real aircraft. There was a fairly strong naval view that such guns would be sufficient and less reliance was placed on fighters which proved a mistake in war conditions. The proportion of fighters was reduced so that when radar became available to detect incoming aircraft, there were no fighters to take advantage of it. In 1936 a committee found that neither the Navy nor the Air Force had scientifically assessed these matters and concluded that anti aircraft fire was not as effective as they had thought. As a result the Admiralty ordered 20mm Oerlikon and 40mm Bofors guns to supplement its ship's anti aircraft capability.

Throughout this period the Navy's carriers took part regularly in the Fleet Exercises. Similar activities were carried out by other major carrier navies of the United States and Japan both of which had grown much faster than the British. They also based their thinking on the battleship and had newer ships than Britain. At the same time they were developing the concept of a Carrier Task Force which could operate independently with suitable escorts. When Rear Admiral Reeves USN used SARATOGA independently and successfully in the 1929 Fleet Exercises, his fresh thinking was not immediately appreciated but he showed the success it could achieve and ultimately did in the Pacific war. The Japanese developed long range high performance aircraft for their carrier task forces which with highly trained aircrews became the spearhead of their conquests in 1941 and 1942.

1918-1939. The Difficult Years.

Ships and Aircraft.

FURIOUS with exhaust smoke coming from vents at the stern.

By the end of World War 1 the Royal Navy had the largest fleet of aircraft and seaplane carriers in the world. Work was proceeding to modify some and there were others that were being converted from existing hulls.

By this time the Navy had acquired a fair amount of experience on the problems of operating aircraft at sea but were not convinced in which direction to move. The main problems experienced so far were: the difficulties of aircraft landing on ships due to the disturbed air flow created by the superstructure, the provision of an efficient method of aircraft control once it was on the deck and the speed of the ship so that it could keep up with the Battle Fleet. There were differences of opinion on the vulnerability of carriers and how to defend them from attacks by aircraft and ships using armour, guns or fighter aircraft. It was to be many years before these problems were resolved and there were limitations because of the reluctance of the Government to spend money after a long and expensive war, followed by the economic depression of the nineteen thirties.

FURIOUS after the trials at the closing stages of the war, was laid up pending a decision on deck changes. ARGUS was commissioned in September 1918 with a complete flush deck with exhaust gases from the engines exiting from either side of the stern of the ship. This method was extremely complex and there were thoughts that it might reduce the efficiency of the engines. The flush deck allowed aircraft to take off and land, all using the same deck space. The other alternative still being considered was to have the exhaust gases from the engines using funnels located in an island type superstructure on the side of the flight deck. Aircraft trials on ARGUS concentrated on the arrester gear and the final solution was to have the longitudinal wires 300 feet in length. The wires would be raised at the touchdown point by a powered ramp that could be lowered for take off. The wires were supported by 15 inch hinged flaps at about 50 feet intervals at the forward end by another ramp that was power operated. The deck between was lower than at either end. This undulating deck can be seen in the photographs. There were also power operated palisades to prevent aircraft from falling over the side. These palisades were long beams projecting from the side of the ship, all connected with netting. Normally the palisades were in the low position almost level with the flight deck. There was a raised trip wire on each side of the flight deck, if the aircraft ran over the trip wire the palisades were automatically raised to the high position about sixty degrees from the horizontal. At this time aircraft were still not provided with wheel brakes. The shape of the round down at the rear of the flight deck was also modified to curve downwards to reduce the amount of disturbed air at the end of the flight deck. The trials of the arrester system completed in the 1921 spring cruise were completely satisfactory.

The completion of the new carriers EAGLE and HERMES was delayed by the general cut back in the armed forces after the war and also because the problem of landing on had not been solved. There were still difficulties with exhaust fumes from ARGUS which discharged them astern and its ducts under the deck overheated. EAGLE which was originally laid down as a Chilean battleship, was used for trials before completion and successful landings and take offs were carried out. Wind tunnel experiments also suggested changes to her island on the starboard side. This also delayed HERMES which was the first ship designed from the start as a carrier and also with a starboard island. Both ships were only commissioned in February 1924 and with speeds of only 24 and 26 knots respectively were too slow to operate with the fleet, as indeed was ARGUS. FURIOUS with a speed of 30 knots was not recommissioned until August 1925. Her sister ships the battle cruisers COURAGEOUS and GLORIOUS were converted into

FURIOUS. Two sunken positions for flying and ship control on either side of the flight deck. Flycatcher in position to fly off from the hangar deck. The wind break is up.

carriers with islands and commissioned in May 1928 and March 1930 respectively. EAGLE and HERMES had flight decks running the complete length of the ship, whereas in the converted FURIOUS, COURAGEOUS and GLORIOUS the flight deck did not extend the full length of the hull.

There was a length of deck between the hangar and the bow of the ship and this was used to launch aircraft directly from the hangar area. The aircraft was held on a quick release system until the engine had obtained full power and then released. This method gradually went out of use as the required take off distance increased due to rising weight of the more modern aircraft.

FURIOUS 1927/28. Ship Conning house in up position. Palisades fitted. Engine exhaust points can be seen at the stern.

The completely flush deck on FURIOUS created problems with the control of the ship and the conduct of flying operations. The solution was to have a retractable conning house in the middle of the forward end of the flight deck, which would be lowered when flying was taking place. When this happened the conning of the ship and control of the aircraft was transferred to two conning positions either side of the flight deck, the tops of which were only just above deck level.

It was in the early 1920's that the longitudinal arrester gear on the carriers was removed. The method had never been popular with the pilots and with the increasing length of the flight decks the aircraft were able to stop without brakes. The problem of the aircraft being blown over the side once they had stopped was partially solved (not always successfully) by the use of the palisades and active flight deck handling crews who manhandled the aircraft to the lifts.

A major step concerning ship safety was made during the post war deliberations that with the new construction the ships' hangars should be of sealed construction. This meant that the danger of fires due to the use of high octane fuel was reduced. There were also fire screens placed at intervals along the length of the hangar. Although good for safety this type of construction had the effect of reducing the width of the hangars and it is for this reason that the numbers of aircraft on board the British carriers were much less than the American carriers that had an open hangar which projected over the side of the ship.

The armament of the British carriers during this period was the subject of long debate and varied between a large number of 6 inch or 4 inch guns, torpedo tubes both above and below the water line and various numbers of smaller guns for protection against aircraft and fewer guns where sufficient space was a problem. The increasing width of the flight decks created problems for the delivery of shells to the larger guns. Guns mounted on the sides of the flight deck would have created blast problems to any aircraft that was on deck at the time.

In 1926 the trials with catapults that had been abandoned during the war were restarted. Various methods of propulsion were tried, a large flywheel, cordite, compressed air or the ship's hydraulic system. It was hoped that the carrier would be able to launch aircraft without having to turn into wind, out of the fleet formation. The early catapults and accelerators were only able to provide part of the aircraft's minimum flying speed, the remainder being supplied by the forward motion of the ship and the actual wind. Later the catapults were able to accelerate the aircraft to flying speed. The Royal Navy called the device an accelerator when it was installed on a carrier and a catapult when on a ship, although later the second term was generally used. The catapults on ships were the first used as the aircraft were getting heavier and could no longer make a free take off from the small platform. An accelerator was initially installed on GLORIOUS in 1928 as a trial. The reaction from the operators was not very favourable. At one time both the Mediterranean and Atlantic Fleet C-in-Cs objected and the installation was removed. Initially the aircraft on ships had to be accelerated with the tail in the flying position and the aircraft supported on a trolley but as the strength of aircraft fuselages increased special spools were installed that allowed the aircraft to be launched in the tail down position. It was on the 26 November 1929 that the first night deck landing was made on COURAGEOUS by a Fairey Flycatcher. In 1935 an accelerator was installed in GLORIOUS and unmanned Fairey IIIF aircraft were used to test the system. From then on most carriers were fitted with two accelerators at the forward end of the flight deck. This enabled reconnaissance aircraft to be launched without the ship leaving the formation.

GLORIOUS accelerator trials with unmanned Fairey IIIF. 28/11/35

GLORIOUS. The undulating flight deck still remains after the removal of the longitudinal arrester wires. Palisades have been fitted

GLORIOUS. After refit in 1938. Two accelerators have been fitted at the bow. New type palisades have been fitted as well as new armament of the hangar flight

COURAGEOUS. 1935/36.
Distinctive island appearance. Two bow accelerators. forward lift marked. Type 72 homing beacon fitted at the top of the main mast.

Blackburn Shark Mk.II No.4356. from 820 Squadron taking off between the two accelerators. Wind deflector down. Possibly GLORIOUS.

In 1930 trials were completed on FURIOUS with seaplanes with metal floats taking off from the flight deck and also the aircraft landing back on, causing spectacular spark displays. Hydraulic wheel brakes were fitted for the first time to late production models of the Fairey Flycatcher. This improved the landing performance of the aircraft. The final solution of how to stop landing-on aircraft was taken when a transverse arrester wire was fitted to GLORIOUS in 1931. This wire operated on a friction drum principle to avoid a sudden deceleration being applied to the aircraft. The initial installation was too far aft so it was moved further forward and more wires installed. The friction device was later changed to a hydraulic controlled drum with compensation for off centre engagements. With the installation of the arrester wires it was possible to provide a parking area forward. To prevent damage by an aircraft missing the wire a barrier was used. This was not immediately popular with pilots because if the parking area was being used with the barrier raised and the aircraft missed the wire, it was not possible to overshoot and make another attempt. Damage to the aircraft and more importantly to the pilot was possible with a barrier engagement.

The aircraft were fitted with a V shaped construction that had a hook at the end of the V. The arrester hook was positioned towards the rear of the aircraft and could be raised and lowered. As it was towards the rear of the aircraft there was less tendency for the aircraft to tip onto its nose when it engaged the wire.

To improve the standard of approaches and to avoid too many barrier engagements the American method of having a batsman to give instructions to the pilot concerning speed, attitude and angle of descent was adopted in 1937. Again there was resistance from pilots who considered that instructions might be given to them by an officer who was junior in rank to them. As more landings were made using this system confidence increased and it became standard procedure until it was superseded by the mirror landing aid.

The Washington Naval Disarmament Conference of 1921 had resulted in a Treaty which gave Britain and America parity of 135,000 tons for aircraft carriers. On the basis that the Navy scrapped the old ARGUS, EAGLE and HERMES and kept FURIOUS, COURAGEOUS and GLORIOUS, 68,000 tons remained for new ships. A Tentative Ten Year Programme was put forward in 1925 for four smaller ships of 17,000 tons each and a speed of 30 knots. It was hoped that the first would be laid down in 1936 and the others at three year intervals after but even the start of the first one was continually put off for economic and political reasons including the 10 Year Rule that there was not likely to be a major war for 10 years. Indeed it was to be 10 years before a new carrier was started in 1936. There was also the difficulty that the Air Ministry which provided the aircraft and much of the personnel considered that carriers were vulnerable and not the best way of providing the air needs of the fleet.

In 1931 discussion began again by the Naval staff on the replacement carriers that would be required for the fleet in preparation for the Geneva Disarmament Conference. The carrier was now becoming a very complex ship and amongst the subjects discussed were: the number of aircraft, type of hangar, length of flight deck, position and size of the island superstructure, number and size of aircraft lifts, defensive weapons, armour protection, number and power of the catapults, range and speed of the ship and the final tonnage of the ship. This last matter was very much affected by the various treaty amendments that were being negotiated, in all not a very easy problem. The Air Staff (RAF) were concerned that the aircraft lifts should be designed for the heavier monoplane aircraft that would be developed

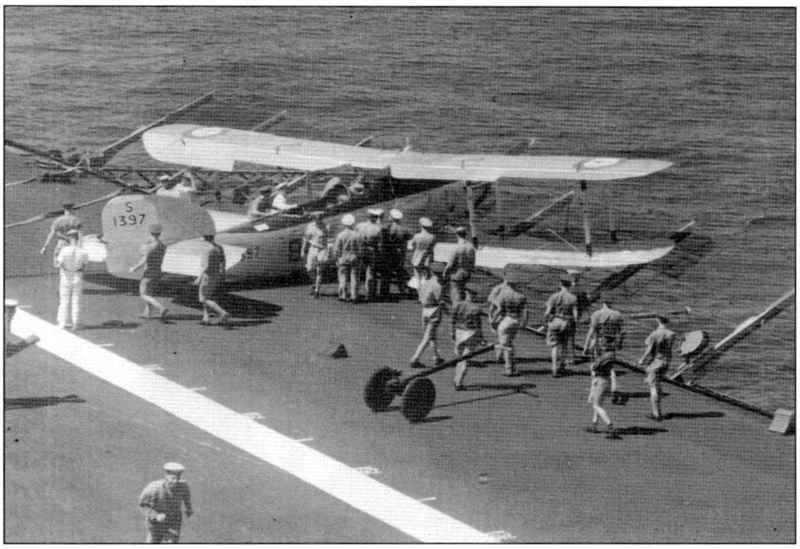

Fairey IIIF. Making use of the palisades. Aircraft would otherwise have been lost overboard.

GLORIOUS. Swordfish Mk.I. K5940 of 825 Squadron using the transverse arrester wires. Hook still engaged with the wire. Upward slope of the forward flight deck still in position.

The Batsman at work. These photographs were taken during WW2. One of the Swordfish is fitted with rocket rails.

Left
TOO HIGH.

Right
CLOSE THROTTLE

in the future. As these were expected to be larger and with an increased performance a new carrier with a long expected life had to be able to keep up with aeronautical progress. The Navy thought that it might be preferable to have a larger number of lower performance aircraft than a smaller number of those with a high performance. It had been thought that the new monoplanes would require more space and more hangar height but this problem was solved when it was realised that the monoplanes usually had a shorter wing span and the wings could be folded. Stronger lifts were needed to take the increased weight of the modern aircraft.

In 1932 the Admiralty put forward proposals for five new carriers of 22,000 tons, carrying 60 aircraft each and with a speed of 30 knots. The Geneva conference did not reach agreement and it became clear that Germany was going to rearm. The proposal for the new ARK ROYAL was put forward for the 1934 building programme but opposed by the Air Ministry which still had no faith in carriers and did not want to increase the FAA in size. Approval was given and ARK ROYAL started in 1936 and completed in 1938, a most impressive ship with a flight deck 720 feet long, two catapults, barriers and arrester wires. She could carry 60 aircraft. This was the first British aircraft carrier to be built with a hangar as an integral part of the ship, serving as the upper strength member.

Armoured flight decks had been a requirement of the Admiralty for some time but the decision for their introduction had been held up until the outcome of the London Naval Conference of 1935-36. It had been decided that the minimum requirement was for four of the new type armoured flight deck carriers. The first two of these,ILLUSTRIOUS and VICTORIOUS were laid down in 1937 the other pair FORMIDABLE and INDOMITABLE were ordered in the 1937 Estimates. All these carriers were to have an armoured hangar and flight deck. The amount and strength of the armour varied between the four carriers. One major outcome of the armoured deck and hangar was the smaller aircraft capacity. In the opinion of the Admiralty this smaller number of aircraft could be achieved by reducing the number of fighter aircraft and relying on the ships' anti-aircraft armament to deal with attacking aircraft. To this end up to eight 4.5in twin guns were fitted as well as six 2pdr pom-pom. Aircraft capacity was about thirty six. These ships were to have catapults capable of launching aircraft with the ship at anchor.

A further two armoured deck carriers INDEFATIGABLE and IMPLACABLE were ordered for 1939 to 1942 and these could carry more aircraft than the earlier ones. The Admiralty justified the armour on these ships as a requirement for operations in the North Sea and the Mediterranean where it was likely to be operating in a war with Germany. This decision was justified in World War 2 against the Germans in the Mediterranean and the Japanese in the Pacific. The driving force behind the carrier programme was Admiral R.G.H.Henderson the Third Sea Lord and Controller who championed the FAA throughout the inter war years.

As part of the building programme the Navy included UNICORN a repair and supply ship with normal flight deck and appropriate facilities for operating aircraft. This was planned to support the fleet carriers and thus effectively increase the number of aircraft available. Unfortunately wartime demands on shipbuilding delayed her completion until March 1943.

The Naval Staff also prepared plans for seven Trade Protection carriers of 14,500 tons and each carrying 14 amphibious aircraft but these had a lower priority and none were started before war broke out in 1939. It was generally felt that underwater detection (ASDIC) would solve the submarine menace to merchant ships when fitted in the escorting vessels. The major problem was defence against surface raiders for which naval surface ships were needed, though shipborne aircraft were needed to search and find the raiders first. There were also objections from the Air Ministry which was reluctant to support any demand for aircraft which might reduce its offensive bomber force.

Though the FAA was catching up with its new carrier building it was still way behind in its aircraft. From 300 attached to the fleet at the end of World War 1 the number soon dropped to 100 or less and this was expected to rise to 150 when COURAGEOUS and GLORIOUS were in use. Financial cutbacks kept even the projected numbers low as late as 1938 and 1942 was the planning date for war with 480 aircraft of which 300 would be in the seven new fleet carriers. In fact at the beginning of the war in 1939 the FAA had only 218 front line aircraft. These were 147 torpedo/strike/reconnaissance (TSR), 41 amphibians and 30 fighters. Another 192 planes were shore based. These numbers were far less than either America or Japan so that the Royal Navy could not possibly match the large attacking forces which these countries were able to use.

GLORIOUS. Blackburn Shark with arrester hook retracted after landing with deck handling crew in control. Aircraft fitted with wheel brakes by this time.

The planes used in the 1920s were the delightful single seat fighter the Flycatcher with the ugly Avro Bison and the Blackburn Blackburn three seaters for reconnaissance and the Blackburn Dart as torpedo carrier. Biplanes continued as standard throughout the 1930s. The Hawker Nimrod replaced the Flycatcher and the Hawker Osprey replaced the popular Fairey 111F three seat spotter. The Fairey Swordfish entered service in GLORIOUS in July 1936 as a three seat TSR and became a legend during the war when the "Stringbag" crippled the BISMARK, sank the Italian fleet at Taranto and helped win the battle of the Atlantic.

The provision of aircraft for both the Navy and the Airforce was beset with problems during the 1930s. There was lack of development due to financial backing due to The Ten Year rule especially as aircraft technology was at the stage where aircraft orders were essential if progress was to be made. Neither of the services helped the situation.

The Air Force was still not convinced that the monoplane was going to be the aircraft of the future, especially as the biplanes with the inline engines that were available were still showing signs of increasing performance. The expectations of available engine power were still only in the region of 1000hp.

The Navy had a different problem altogether. Their requirement was for aircraft that could land at slow speeds and the biplane was one of these. Naval requirements also called for aircraft that could satisfy several different roles and for this the aircraft needed several crew members. This meant that the aircraft were heavy as compared with the Air Force counterpart. However the engine power remained the same so performance was lower, also the Navy preferred radial engines which had greater reliability.

Higher powered engines were under development at the end of the 1930s but with the rapid rearmament programme engines were in short supply and most of the production went to the Air Force for use in the rapidly expanding fighter force.

For the naval single seat fighters the problem was the ability of the aircraft to find the carrier on completion of the mission. The standard procedure was to send a two seat aircraft with the fighters so that the observer could navigate the formation back to the carrier. Aircraft operating in the Mediterranean carried out regular flights of over 400 miles and were able to return to within an average error of 12 miles, from where the aircraft were expected to complete a visual rejoin. In daylight in areas where the weather was good this was satisfactory but at night or if the weather was bad a problem existed especially if fuel was short.

There was a Direction Finding facility when the carrier was with the fleet which could provide an approximate heading back home. Later there was available a beacon that could be fitted on the carrier that would have enabled the aircraft to find the carrier. This system found little favour with the fleet as it would have also directed the enemy as well.

Despite having single seat fighters, the navy decided that it would be better served with two seaters which would enable them to carry an observer for navigation. In the absence of homing devices it was often difficult for pilots to find the carrier when returning. It would also help in escorting bombers to distant targets. The first monoplane designed for the FAA was also specified as a dive bomber, the Blackburn Skua, but it was too slow as a fighter and only carried one 500lb bomb. Nevertheless Skuas sank the KONIGSBERG in Bergen during the Norwegian campaign and later in the war fighters were used for bombing attacks. The variant Roc two seater fighter with a gun turret was never used on carriers and the Navy had to acquire 50 biplane Gloster Gladiators fighters in May 1939.

And so in September 1939 the FAA went to war with one modern aircraft carrier ARK ROYAL, three converted battlecruisers and three carriers which were too slow and too old. Its aircraft were a modern fighter/dive bomber which was too slow and a biplane TSR maid of all work with an open cockpit and too slow even to catch up with the ship if the wind was strong. It also had few aircrewmen and maintenance personnel.

1939-1945. World War 2.

Pre-War Carriers.

At eleven o'clock on the morning of the 3rd September 1939 the Prime Minister Neville Chamberlain announced on the radio that we were at war with Germany. COURAGEOUS was at anchor at Plymouth and sailed that evening with two Swordfish Squadrons 811 and 822 and escorted by four destroyers to provide anti submarine patrols in the Western Approaches. The Swordfish were sent off to look for submarines. In the evening of 17th September when two of the destroyers were away helping a merchant ship under U boat attack, COURAGEOUS herself was sighted and attacked by U-29. Two torpedoes hit the ship at 1950 and it sank 15 minutes later with the loss of 519 men and all the aircraft about 350 miles west of Land's End. The FAA with ill considered plans and tactics had lost the first of its precious few ships, aircraft and men.

HERMES which had been engaged on similar duties was promptly sent off to West Africa. ARK ROYAL was on similar duties in the North West Approaches and on the 14th September U-39 attacked with two torpedoes which exploded nearby. On the 26th September in the North Sea with the Home Fleet her Skuas shot down a Dornier shadower and drove off two others but not before they had reported the Fleet which was attacked by Heinkels. One bomb dropped just ahead of ARK ROYAL which was severely shaken.

The carriers gave up anti submarine patrols and turned their attention to surface raiders one of which was known to be a German pocket battleship. FURIOUS was in the North Atlantic, HERMES in the West Indies, EAGLE in the East Indies, GLORIOUS near Aden and ARK ROYAL in the South Atlantic where her aircraft flew continuous patrols without finding their quarry. Success fell to Commodore Harwood's Cruiser Squadron of AJAX, ACHILLES and EXETER which sighted and engaged GRAF SPEE with considerable spotting assistance from AJAX's Seafox flown by Lieutenant Lewin. Both sides sustained considerable damage and after several days in Montevideo GRAF SPEE emerged only to be scuttled and blown up.

Skuas of 800/803 Squadrons on ARK ROYAL before theTrondheim raid.

Germany invaded Norway on 9th April 1940 lead by the battlecruisers SCHARNHORST and GNEISENAU and the heavy cruiser HIPPER and landed at several towns on the coast. The Home Fleet which set sail to oppose them had to rely very much on the seaplanes it carried and on 18 Swordfish in FURIOUS which had to leave without its Skua fighter/bombers as they were at a distant air station. ARK ROYAL and GLORIOUS were training in the Mediterranean and were hurriedly recalled. The three carriers and their aircraft were continuously in action up and down the Norwegian coast from Narvik in the north to Stavanger in the south throughout the campaign where they were opposed by the German Fliegerkorps X which outnumbered and had superior aircraft to the FAA. The FAA achieved a major success when on 10th April a force of 15 Skuas from ARK ROYAL's 800 and 803 Squadrons flew from Hatson in the Orkneys on a round trip of 560 miles to dive bomb the light cruiser KONIGSBERG moored in Bergen harbour.

ARGUS below decks hangar. Sea Hurricanes of 768 Squadron.

All the 15x500 lb bombs were hits or near misses and the ship caught fire, turned over and sank. This was the first capital ship to be sunk by dive bombing.

On 11th April Swordfish from FURIOUS made the world's first real torpedo attack against ships in Trondheim but there were only two destroyers and the torpedoes exploded too soon in the shallow water. On the 13th the Swordfish on floats from WARSPITE was crucial to the second attack at Narvik by WARSPITE and destroyers when it warned them of the Germans ships' hidden positions and reported the fall of shot. ARK ROYAL and GLORIOUS arrived at the end of April and flew fighter patrols and support strikes but the Skuas were no match for the German fighters. The two carriers showed the importance of shipborne aircraft in campaigns beyond the range of land based aircraft from Britain but they had neither the numbers nor aircraft of adequate performance.

At the beginning of June it was decided to withdraw from Norway GLORIOUS carrying RAF Hurricanes and Gladiators as well as her own aircraft and the RAF crews, was detached to return to the UK escorted only by two destroyers on 7th June. It was not known that SCHARNHORST and GNEISENAU were patrolling the area and they sighted GLORIOUS the next afternoon, opening fire at 1630. The carrier and her escorts were sunk by gunfire with the loss of all but 43 survivors. One of the destroyers ACASTA had launched her torpedoes and damaged SCHARNHORST before being sunk. The German ship went to Trondheim and 5 days later ARK ROYAL sent 15 Skuas to bomb it in daylight with no cloud cover and Messerschmitts ready for them. There was only one hit and the bomb failed to explode. Eight Skuas were shot down.

The Norwegian campaign had shewn what the FAA and its carriers could do but at the cost of the second of its four fast carriers and the loss of over 100 aircrew.

On the outbreak of war EAGLE moved from the Far East to provide patrols in the East Indies and when Italy joined the war in June 1940 she had replaced GLORIOUS in the Mediterranean and her Swordfish made many raids in North Africa and elsewhere. The Sea Gladiators also proved their worth against Italian aircraft.

Force H and ARK ROYAL returned to the Mediterranean to carry out five convoy escorts and eleven aircraft ferry runs to Malta in which ARGUS and FURIOUS also took part. ARK ROYAL had been reported sunk by Lord Haw Haw on the German radio many times since she was near missed at the start of the war but she had never been hit despite several near misses. On 13th November 1941 her luck ran out when U-81 made a single torpedo hit on the starboard side and she sank before she could reach Gibraltar.

With the loss of ARK ROYAL in November 1941 there was no carrier in Force H in the Western Mediterranean until the old EAGLE joined in March 1942. The sending of aircraft and supplies to Malta was a continual problem and EAGLE and ARGUS were used to ferry in Spitfires to the island. Convoy "Harpoon" was sent in and the carriers' fighters shot down 11 enemy aircraft. EAGLE was with operation "Pedestal" to again supply Malta when on 11th August 1942 she was torpedoed by U-73 and sunk. HERMES had already been sunk by Japanese carrier aircraft off Trincomalee in Ceylon on 8th April 1942. Only FURIOUS and ARGUS of the pre war carriers survived to the end of the war.

VICTORIOUS. Sea Hurricanes of 885 Squadron. Operation Pedestal. Followed by INDOMITABLE and EAGLE.

1939-1945. World War 2.
Trade Protection Carriers.

Between the two world wars the Navy had considered the problems of protecting the shipping that would be needed to provide the country with its food and war supplies. These plans were based on the experiences of World War 1 and the main threat was perceived to be attacks by surface raiders and by submarines. The solution to attacks by surface raiders would be very much the same as in World War 1, the provision of armed merchant ships. However the ability of aircraft to operate from ships would increase the effectiveness of the ships by allowing for air reconnaissance.

It was thought that the submarine problem could be dealt with by the convoy system and land based aircraft as the submarines were expected to operate in the vicinity of and in the approaches to the British Isles.

During the pre-war years the Navy had completed several studies of the type of ships that might be needed for armed merchant cruisers and trade protection carriers.The carriers would be quite large and would be equipped with a full length flight deck, lifts and arrester equipment while the merchant cruisers would be equipped with catapults with two or three aircraft. This meant quite extensive structural alteration and would be expensive. As the money available was needed for more urgent requirements, the idea was abandoned.

In the early days of the war the convoys were protected by naval vessels and by the aircraft of RAF Coastal Command. This command had suffered badly from the lack of financial assistance and was mainly equipped with short range aircraft apart from the few squadrons of Short Sunderland flying boats. The German submarines were now operating further into the Atlantic than had been expected and the convoys were having to be protected by the scarce fleet carriers. As the convoys moved slowly this put the carriers at great risk from submarine attack.

After the fall of France the German submarine fleet was in a much better position to operate further away from attacks by land based aircraft and they could also receive information on the positions of the convoys from reconnaissance aircraft. A new dimension was added when the Focke Wolfe Condor (a military conversion of a four engined civilian aircraft) began to operate far out into the Atlantic on reconnaissance and bombing flights.

In late 1941 both the Navy and the Air Force considered solutions to these problems. One RAF solution was to have some ships equipped as mobile radar stations to control fighter aircraft sent from land. This idea was dropped because the fighter aircraft would take too long to reach the area when enemy aircraft had been sighted. The Deputy Chief of the Air Staff, Air Vice Marshal Sir Sholto Douglas, thought that the provision of several hundred ships, each fitted with a catapult and two or three aircraft would be a solution. It was expected that the air combats would take place within a few hundred miles of land and the aircraft would be able to reach a land base after combat. If this was not possible the aircraft would ditch and the pilot be picked up. There was some resistance to this idea as pilots were more valuable than aircraft and the possible loss of a pilot was something to be avoided.

Sea Hurricane on the catapult of a merchant ship.(C.A.M.). I.W.M.

A major problem arose when the supply of suitable catapults was considered. The ones being delivered were complex and in very short supply, took a long time to build and only five were available at this time. The Navy converted the anti-aircraft ship SPRINGBANK to be the first equipped with one of the catapults. Several catapults were diverted from cruisers then building to equip other anti-aircraft carriers. Several aircraft types were considered and the Hawker Hurricane and the Fairey Fulmar were the aircraft selected. SPRINGBANK would have three Fulmar aircraft on board. While the conversion was being completed PEGASUS (the old ARK ROYAL) which was used as a catapult training ship, was sent with three Fulmars to escort some of the Gibraltar convoys.

The RAF was still very keen to have large numbers of fighters to protect convoys and suggested placing short flying decks on cargo ships. The Hurricane could operate from normal carrier decks but not from the short ones mounted on the bow of a tanker so some type of assisted take off would be required. A breakthrough came when rockets were first used to assist the Hurricane to take off. The Royal Aircraft Establishment at Farnborough had built and successfully tested a rocket catapult before the end of 1940. It was now possible to place catapults on the bows of normal cargo vessels that were still under construction. This method was chosen to avoid the use of vessels that were in service. Thirty five merchant vessels were converted in this way and called Catapult Armed Merchantman (CAM) and joined the convoys from 1941 onwards. They were used on the Atlantic and Arctic convoys and although the number of German aircraft shot down was not large, they were a considerable deterrent and drove off the shadowing aircraft. Initially the aircraft were piloted by FAA pilots until the RAF pilots had received catapult training. The Hawker Hurricane was the principal aircraft used in this role.

It was in December 1941 that the next stage in the provision of aircraft protection for the convoys was made. Captain M.S. Slattery RN suggested that a simple carrier could be made by having a merchant hull with a flat deck that would be equipped with a two wire arrester gear and a barrier. There would be no hangar for the six Hurricane fighters and the ship was also expected to carry cargo. This last requirement would have made the ship too complicated and the ships were to be built without it. These vessels were called Auxiliary Fighter Carriers. The first was a converted captured German prize ship Hannover renamed AUDACITY which was equipped with Grumman Martlet fighters. It was intended that this type of ship should replace the CAM ships as the fighters could land on again. At this stage of the war the German aircraft were operating well out into the Atlantic and the catapulted aircraft stood little chance of being able to get to land once they were launched.

From this adaptation came the Merchant Aircraft Carrier(MAC), this being either a grain ship of about 8000 tons or a tanker of 9000 tons. Both were fitted with a flight deck 400 feet in length and arrester wires and the usual flight operation requirements. The loss of cargo space was minimal. These carried Swordfish aircraft to find and attack submarines with depth charges. Several successful attacks on submarines were made by aircraft from the MAC ships but the main effect was to keep the submarines submerged so that they could not see the convoys and also to reduce the time the submarines had to recharge their batteries. With the introduction of the escort carrier the MAC ship's role was less vital and eventually they were all returned to their normal roles.

With the increasing availabilty of cargo ships in America a new type of aircraft carrier came into use, the escort carrier. In early 1941 America was asked to build for the Royal Navy, six ships of a slightly improved design with an island and a hangar with a lift.One carrier was retained by the US Navy for training new pilots. This design was used in both American and British future construction. Several types of escort carriers were to be used. Some were used for anti submarine purposes and were equipped with Swordfish aircraft; some had both fighter and anti submarine aircraft. There were others that were used for ferrying aircraft and in one short period over two hundred aircraft were delivered from America by this method. There were also assault carriers mainly equipped with fighters and fighter direction systems. The majority were constructed in shipyards in America and were equipped with American Wildcat fighters and the Avenger torpedo bomber/reconnaissance aircraft. The escort carriers were equipped with arrester wires and a single catapult. The American type of catapult required the aircraft to be in a tail down position and this was the reason for using these aircraft. The Swordfish was used on some of the escort carriers as it did not need a catapult launch. The numbers of aircraft varied between fifteen and twenty according to the role of the carrier and type of aircraft.

Rocket catapult launch of Sea Hurricane. I.W.M.

In 1942 the decision was made to convert in Britain two existing armed merchant cruisers and two large fast merchant ships into escort carriers. The largest of these at 17,780 tons was the PRETORIA CASTLE a Union-Castle Line vessel. Several more conversions were made in British yards. These larger ships could carry an average of eighteen aircraft. The ships were more sophisticated in their armour and had six arrester wires and a twin track catapult. They were also fitted for night flying and spent most of their time in Arctic waters.

Later in their service life some of the escort carriers were equipped with Seafire fighters. The escort carrier served in all the theatres of operation during the war, a typical use apart from their convoy protection duties was supporting the invasion of Italy at Salerno.

Responsibility for air cover over the Salerno landing zone was with Force V, consisting of 4 escort carriers and the repair carrier UNICORN on one of her few operational outings, under the command of Admiral Sir Philip Vian. They carried 112 Seafires and were required to maintain a continuous cover of 20 aircraft over the beachhead between dawn and 0830 and between 1630 and dusk, the aircraft being flown off every hour and remaining airborne for 85 minutes. It was expected that

Escort Carrier SEARCHER. Wildcats on deck.

EMPIRE MacCOLL (a MAC ship) with convoy. Swordfish behind wind barriers.

Escort Carrier SEARCHER off Norway in 1944. Note different colours of hull to break up the outline.

Escort Carrier SEARCHER in heavy weather. Spots on the picture are water on the camera lens.

SPRINGBANK with Fairey Fulmar fighter on catapult.

the RAF Spitfires and other fighters would be flying from the airfield at Montecorvino by the end of the first day but it was not captured and the FAA Seafires had to continue for another two days by which time they were running out of aircraft. An airstrip had to be made ashore to which the remaining 26 Seafires were transferred on 12th September and they operated until the crisis was over and they could return to their ships. Carrier air support for amphibious landings had again been proved but the use of a single aircraft type and the Seafire in particular had not been a success. The Seafires were not robust enough for deck landings on escort carriers with their slower speed. The Seafires were also too slow to catch the German fighter bombers and only shot down 2 and damaged 4 in 3 days of combat. 10 were lost to the enemy and 40 were lost in accidents when landing on.

For the landings in the South of France in August 1944 another FAA Task Force was formed with 7 escort carriers and 2 American carriers with 48 Hellcats. The British had 98 Seafires, 49 Wildcats and 22 Hellcats. Their main role was in Army Cooperation, bombardment spotting, tactical reconnaissance and ground attack. They flew 1500 sorties in six days, the Seafires giving short range support and the Wildcats and Hellcats flying inland sweeps.

The carriers in the East Indies Fleet in 1944 were the three escort carriers AMEER, EMPRESS and SHAH which were joined in March 1945 by EMPEROR, HUNTER, KHEDIVE, STALKER and ATTACKER from the Mediterranean to form 21st Aircraft Carrier Squadron. The fleet supplied support for the 14th Army in Burma and was required to contain the Japanese cruisers at Singapore. AMEER's Hellcats gave cover for landings on Ramree Island in January and on Chedduba Island. 888 squadron photo-reconnaissance Hellcats flew from EMPRESS with AMEER providing Combat Air Patrols (CAP) to obtain photo coverage of the Kra Isthmus, Penang and northern Sumatra for use by the 14th Army. EMPEROR and KHEDIVE struck at targets in Sumatra in April and with HUNTER and STALKER covered and supported the landings to occupy Rangoon in early May. SHAH and EMPRESS with the 3rd Battle Squadron were covering against possible interference by the Japanese cruisers at Singapore and attacked airfields and harbours in the Andaman and Nicobar Islands as well as the Burmese coast. All units were back in Trincomalee on the 9th May the day after Victory in Europe Day.

The following morning SHAH, EMPEROR, HUNTER and KHEDIVE sailed with the 3rd Battle Squadron and the 26th Destroyer Flotilla as a submarine in the Malacca Strait had sighted the Japanese cruiser HAGURO and three escorts heading northwest. At dawn on the 15th 4 Avengers were sent on a search to maximum depth and two further searches followed resulting in the sighting of HAGURO just before noon over 200 miles from the carriers. There were only three Avengers available for a strike which dive bombed HAGURO at 1605 dropping 12 x 500lb semi armour piercing bombs but only making a near miss. HAGURO was clearly making back to Singapore and was caught and sunk that night in a classic night torpedo attack by the 26th Destroyer Flotilla.

21st Aircraft Carrier Squadron continued to operate offensively and covered the reoccupation of Malaya and Singapore. They were credited with destroying more than a third of the serviceable enemy aircraft in Burma, Malaya and Sumatra over a six month period.

View from Observers cockpit on the approach to a MAC ship. Aircraft parked on the other side of the barrier. Pick up the arrester wire or hit the barrier!

1939-1945. World War 2.

Fleet Armoured Carriers.

At the outbreak of the war the Royal Navy had under construction four carriers of the ILLUSTRIOUS Class and two of the IMPLACABLE Class, all having armoured decks.

These ships had been the result of the large rearmament programme that began in 1936. The main thrust of naval tactics at this time was still the use of heavy gun engagement between fleets. Fortunately there were some people in the Admiralty who could see the way in which aircraft carriers could be used in a future war.

The design of this new class of carriers took into account that in a future war the aircraft carrier would be operating mainly in the North Sea, Western approaches and the Mediterranean. In these areas the carriers could expect to be attacked by land based aircraft that would have a superior performance to carrier aircraft. Also the decision had been made that the carrier should rely on its own armament to repel air attacks, the main use of its own aircraft would be to find and attack enemy shipping.

It was for these reasons that the new carriers would have armoured flight decks so that they could withstand enemy bombing. The intention was that the ships would have only one hangar whose roof should be armoured with up to 3½ inches of armour, the sides having a slightly thicker armour. If the ships had been of normal layout with two hangar decks this extra weight would have caused a rather unstable vessel so there was to be only one hangar and this would be part of the structure of the ship. An important consideration was that the hangar was to be completely enclosed with a ventilation system to draw off petrol fumes. This proved to be a major asset when the carriers received bomb damage and no British carrier was lost due to fire or explosion unlike some of the American carriers. This method of hangar construction was to be used in British carriers in the future. Due to the smaller hangar space the carrier could carry only 36 aircraft as compared with the 54 of the ARK ROYAL. The Admiralty was concerned that if the numbers of aircraft were made public there would be a comparison made with the ARK ROYAL and the secret of the armoured deck would be revealed. Therefore in calculating the number of aircraft that could be carried, the numbers that could be carried on the deck without interfering with flying operations were included. This brought the published number of aircraft to the same as ARK ROYAL.

The armour plated deck was designed to withstand hits by 500lb armour piercing bombs. For self defence a very heavy armament was carried including a large

ILLUSTRIOUS. June 1942. Front aircraft Fulmar Mk.IIs of 806 Squadron. Rear aircraft Marlet IIs of 881 Squadron. Battleship WARSPITE firing main guns.

number of 4.5inch guns and 20mm cannon. The main armament reduced the width of the flight deck at either end and limited the number of aircraft that could be parked. The flight deck sloped down at the rear of the carrier (the round down) to avoid generating turbulence for landing aircraft. As this reduced the usable flight deck by some 120 feet, later in the war this slope was removed and the full length restored. Radar of various types was included in these carriers.

The first of the class ILLUSTRIOUS was commissioned in 1940 followed in order by FORMIDABLE (Nov 1940), VICTORIOUS (May 1941) and INDOMITABLE (Oct 1941).

ILLUSTRIOUS joined the Fleet in September 1940 with Swordfish and the new Fairey Fulmar two seat fighter which was replacing the Skua. With a speed of only 240 mph it was still too slow against single seat German fighters but its eight machine guns were a great improvement and more than enough against Italian shadowing and strike aircraft. The arrival of this new ship enabled a planned attack on the Italian Fleet to be put into effect. Photographic reconnaissance by the RAF confirmed the presence of five battleships in harbour at Taranto on the south coast of Italy. ILLUSTRIOUS sailed from Alexandria on the morning of the 11th November 1940 and her aircraft included five from EAGLE which had a fuel problem and could not go. The first wave of 12 Swordfish, 6 with torpedoes, 4 with bombs and 2 with flares left at 2100 and the second wave of 8 aircraft an hour later with torpedoes and bombs. There was no surprise and the aircraft were met with heavy flak(anti aircraft fire) and a balloon barrage. The flares lit up the harbour and torpedoes were launched against the battleships whilst the bombers attacked shore installations. Two aircraft were shot down and one crew was taken prisoner. CAVOUR was sunk and LITTORIO and CAIO DUILLO were severely damaged and out of service for nearly a year.

On 10th January 1941 while covering a convoy to Malta, ILLUSTRIOUS was attacked by Ju87 dive bombers and was hit and severely damaged by six 500kg armour piercing bombs and three near misses. The ship managed to reach Malta where it was bombed and hit again before sailing on the 23rd for Suez and the United States for major repairs. She was replaced in March by the newly completed FORMIDABLE the second ship of the class. On 27th March a RAF Sunderland sighted the Italian Fleet and the British Fleet gave chase off Matapan. FORMIDABLE's Albacores found the enemy and torpedoed the battleship VITTORIO VENETO but it was able to make repairs and escape. They also hit and stopped a cruiser POLA. Two other cruisers ZARA and FIUME and two destroyers stayed with POLA not knowing the British Fleet was near. The Italian ships were caught and sunk by the battleships WARSPITE, VALIANT and BARHAM.

On 25th May FORMIDABLE was assisting in the defence of Crete with a successful raid on Scarpanto and in the afternoon was attacked by 30 Ju87 dive bombers. Her Fulmars shot down four but the ship was hit by two 500kg armour piercing bombs and damaged by a near miss. Repairs were too much to be done at Alexandria and she sailed to join her sister ship ILLUSTRIOUS in America. Her Squadrons remained ashore in the desert where their navigational skills assisted the RAF operating in the desert and enabled them to provide the first "pathfinder" service for the RAF bombers. There was no other carrier to serve with the Eastern Mediterranean Fleet.

The armoured carrier had proved its worth. The American Navy were very impressed that the ships could survive this amount of damage and it influenced the design of some of their later carriers.

The third armoured carrier VICTORIOUS completed her sea trials in April 1941 and on 15th May set sail for Malta with 48 crated Hurricanes. She also carried 9 Swordfish of 825 Squadron and 6 Fulmars of 800 for the defence of the ship on passage but the crews were without recent torpedo strike training. The German battleship BISMARCK was at Bergen in Norway ready to go into the Atlantic to attack British shipping. On 22nd May Commander Hank Rotherham with Lieutenant Commander Noel Goddard as pilot flew a Maryland in atrocious weather from Hatson to Bergen and confirmed that BISMARCK had sailed. The Home Fleet immediately put to sea and VICTORIOUS was diverted to join the fleet as no other carrier was available.

BISMARCK was found by the cruisers SUFFOLK and NORFOLK and the latter's Walrus shadowed the enemy for the next two days during which there was a running battle between BISMARCK with PRINZ EUGEN and HOOD and PRINCE OF WALES resulting in the loss of the HOOD and damage to the PRINCE OF WALES. Despite a 32 feet swell Lieutenant Commander Eugene Esmonde took off from VICTORIOUS with his 9 Swordfish to make a night torpedo attack on BISMARCK at midnight on the 24th and made one hit amidships. They all returned safely but 2 Fulmars which were shadowing were lost and only one crew was picked up. The enemy was lost in the bad weather for over a day and by then was out of range for VICTORIOUS's aircraft.

Swordfish taking off from VICTORIOUS to attack BISMARCK.

BISMARCK was getting short of fuel as the hit from the PRINCE OF WALES had damaged her fuel tanks and turned for Brest in France, a move anticipated by the Admiralty which had ordered Force H up north from Gibraltar. This included ARK ROYAL whose searching Swordfish spotted BISMARCK shortly after it had been found by an RAF Catalina. A strike of 12 Swordfish was launched with the deck rising and falling over 50 feet in heavy seas but unfortunately they attacked SHEFFIELD by mistake in the bad visibility but with no hits. A second strike made a radar assisted attack and 11 torpedoes were dropped, one hitting BISMARCK amidships and another aft causing the rudders to jam and damaging the propellers. This sealed her fate and she was sunk by gunfire and torpedoes from the battleships, cruisers and destroyers. Aircraft from VICTORIOUS and EAGLE subsequently found and sank three German supply ships.

Albacores of 827 and 828 Squadrons on VICTORIOUS for the Kirkenes raid.

In July 1941 after the German attack on Russia FURIOUS and VICTORIOUS made strikes against Kirkenes and Petsamo in Norway and once again the Fulmars were outclassed by the Me 109s but nevertheless shot down some of them.

While the four ships of the ILLUSTRIOUS class were under construction thought was given to the limited aircraft capacity and INDOMITABLE was completed with a half length hangar aft below the main hangar. The height of the upper hangar had to be reduced to accommodate this. The ship could now stow 48 aircraft below decks and parking on the flight deck could increase the total to 54 aircraft.

IMPLACABLE was commissioned in August 1944 and the sister ship INDEFATIGABLE in May 1944. These ships were extensively modified from the ILLUSTRIOUS Class and included an upper and lower hangar, a longer flight deck and accommodation for 81 aircraft with flight deck parking. This larger number of aircraft required a larger ship's crew, spares and stores so the forward part of the lower hangar was converted to extra accommodation.

The aircraft carrier had a very important role in the Mediterranean area in the supply of aircraft for the Royal Air Force. The demands on the Royal Air Force for the defence of Malta and for support for the Army in the Western Desert were very great and it was difficult to supply the fighters due to the distance between possible landing fields. Large numbers of aircraft were ferried by carriers to West Africa from where they were flown overland. Other carriers at great loss to themselves carried a large number of fighters with RAF pilots to within flying range of Malta. Most of these flights were led by FAA aircraft to provide navigational assistance. In the years leading up to the victories in North Africa some 700 aircraft were delivered in this manner.

Meanwhile the type of aircraft available to the Fleet in the Mediterranean was slowly changing. Initially the carriers were equipped mainly with the Swordfish, Albacore and Skua for offensive operations and the Fulmar fighter for Fleet and strike aircraft defence. By 1942 the reduction in Naval aircraft production during the Battle of Britain was taking effect. Despite great efforts by their crews the Fulmar with its low performance was increasingly threatened by the high performance German fighters and bombers that were now being used. An attempt was made to redress the balance by using Hurricane and Martlet fighters. The Hurricane with its large wing span was suitable for carrier operation but was unable to use the lifts on some carriers and had to remain on deck. Even the Hurricane did not have the performance required to combat the enemy aircraft. The planned replacement for the FAA, the Firefly, was well behind schedule so the only possible replacement apart from American aircraft was the Spitfire. It was known that this aircraft with its narrow track undercarriage would have difficulty on the carrier but it was the only aircraft that had the performance. The first of the Seafires (Spitfire) were used on the carriers in 1942 and later

RAF Hurricane fighters with long range tanks on VICTORIOUS for ferrying to Malta spring 1942.

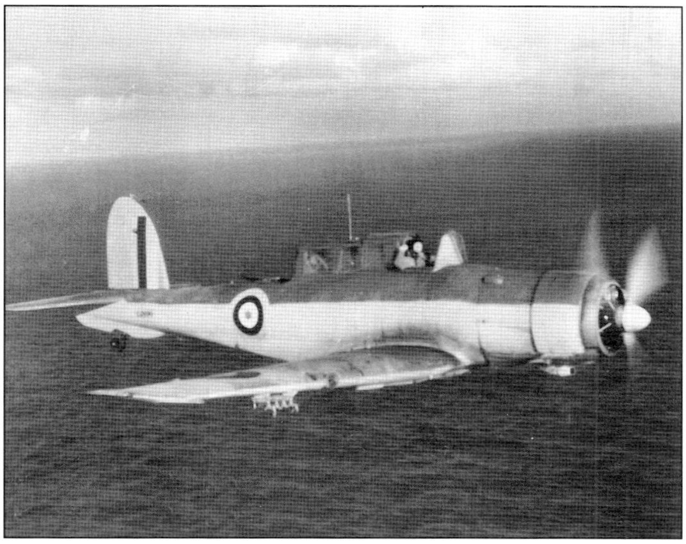
Blackburn Skua.

HERMES.

versions had folding wings so that they could use the aircraft lifts. As demonstrated at Salerno providing there was sufficient wind over the deck and the pilots were familiar with the aircraft, the aircraft could be used on carriers. In many of the operations the Seafires were fitted with bombs for dive bombing attacks. Increasing numbers of Martlet and Hellcat aircraft were also used in later operations.

In December 1941 disaster struck in the Far East when early on the morning of 7th Japanese carriers launched torpedo and bomb attacks on the American Fleet at Pearl Harbor destroying most of it. Luckily the USN carriers were at sea and remained to wreak retribution six months later. The Japanese also attacked southwards in many places including Siam and Malaya and the Royal Navy's PRINCE OF WALES and REPULSE were caught off Malaya without fighter protection and sunk by land based aircraft with torpedoes and bombs. The new carrier INDOMITABLE should have been there but had been delayed when she went aground working up off Jamaica and had to be repaired in America.

A new Eastern Fleet was formed under Admiral Sir James Somerville and included three carriers, INDOMITABLE, FORMIDABLE now repaired and HERMES. The Japanese Admiral Nagumo with five carriers and over 300 aircraft attacked Colombo in Ceylon on 5th April 1942 but little damage was done. Later that day they found and sank the British cruisers DORSETSHIRE and CORNWALL. Aircraft from INDOMITABLE sighted some of the Japanese carriers late in the day but contact was lost. On the 8th the enemy struck at Trincomalee and found HERMES which had been ordered to sea. She had neither her own nor land based RAF fighters to defend her and was sunk. The Japanese went back to the Pacific to carry out plans to destroy the American carriers but they were defeated at the battles of the Coral Sea in May and at Midway in June. In these two engagements between two carrier strike forces, only the aircrews saw the enemy ships which were about 100 miles apart.

Because of concern that the Vichy French might allow Japanese bases in the Island of Madagascar off the East African Coast, an amphibious assault was planned covered by ILLUSTRIOUS which now had American Grumman Martlet fighters and Swordfish and INDOMITABLE with Fulmars and Albacores. During the three days of the operation 309 sorties were flown from the two carriers which established air supremacy and enabled this first amphibious operation with only carrier based air support to succeed.

VICTORIOUS still with the Home Fleet, escorted a convoy to Russia in August and September 1941 followed by attacks on shipping in Norwegian waters. In March she covered convoy PQ12 and also had trials with the new Seafires which had difficulties in operating from carriers. On 9th March 1942 the German battleship TIRPITZ and sister to BISMARK was found and attacked with torpedoes by Albacores from VICTORIOUS but unfortunately no hits were made and a further opportunity did not occur. It did however lead Hitler to decree that the ship was not to put to sea if a carrier was likely to oppose it. On 27th June VICTORIOUS sailed from Iceland to escort the ill fated convoy PQ17 which was scattered and the escorts withdrawn so that 22 merchant ships were sunk, 14 by aircraft and there were no carrier borne aircraft to deter them.

The Malta situation again being desperate convoy "Pedestal" was mounted in mid August 1942. The 14 fast merchant ships were escorted by 2 battleships, 7 cruisers, 20 destroyers and 3 fleet carriers, VICTORIOUS from the Home Fleet, INDOMITABLE from the Eastern Fleet and EAGLE. They had 70 fighters and another 6 on FURIOUS which was ferrying 38 Spitfires. On the afternoon of 11th August when FURIOUS was flying off the Spitfires, EAGLE was hit by 4 torpedoes from U-73 and sank within minutes. The fighters broke up the continuing enemy air attacks and though VICTORIOUS was hit the bomb broke up on the armoured deck. The carriers were attacked again by over 100 aircraft by which time the defending fighters were down to half their original strength and INDOMITABLE was hit twice and also holed by a near miss but her armoured deck saved her though she had to go to America for repairs.

37 aircraft were shot down for the loss of 13 fighters. Five ships reached Malta including the tanker OHIO and Malta was saved. FURIOUS made two more trips to fly off Spitfires to Malta.

For the Allied amphibious landings in North Africa in November 1942 the FAA provided 3 fleet carriers FORMIDABLE, VICTORIOUS and FURIOUS: also ARGUS and 3 escort carriers BITER, DASHER and AVENGER. There were 130 fighters and 30 torpedo bombers. The Americans had off the Moroccan coast 5 carriers with 120 fighters and 63 torpedo bombers. The airfields in the Algiers section were soon taken with the help of the FAA strikes against airfields and coastal defences. At Oran the FAA provided initial cover for the American landing forces. Most of the aircraft were destroyed on the ground and there were also successes in combat. The fleet carriers provided cover against possible intervention by the Italian Fleet but this did not materialise. Whilst covering the withdrawing convoys AVENGER was torpedoed and sunk by U-155 on 15th November.

The next Allied landings were on the 10th July 1943 in Sicily with FORMIDABLE and INDOMITABLE providing a covering force in case the Italian Fleet should appear which it did not. On the next day they were surprised by a Ju88 which torpedoed INDOMITABLE having been mistaken for a returning Albacore. Again the ship went off to America for repairs. For the landings at Salerno in Italy FORMIDABLE and ILLUSTRIOUS provided cover but on the 9th September the Italian Fleet surrendered.

Fleet carriers took part in operations against German shipping and installations in Norway in 1944 and 1945 till the war ended. FURIOUS was always there and VICTORIOUS, FORMIDABLE, INDEFATIGABLE and IMPLACABLE all made appearances. TIRPITZ was a continuing threat to the British Fleet and convoys but would not venture out. The ship had been damaged by midget submarines in September 1943 at Kaa fjord and FAA attacks were made in April, July and August 1944. In April the first strike by 21 Barracudas of 8 TBR wing from FURIOUS and VICTORIOUS surprised TIRPITZ at 0530 as she was getting under way and a second strike by Barracudas of 52 TBR Wing attacked an hour later. The dive bombers made 14 hits causing considerable damage and loss of life as well as damaging three other ships. Two aircraft were lost. The escorting fighters, Corsairs, Wildcats, Hellcats and Seafires from both the fleet and escort carriers, EMPEROR, PURSUER, SEARCHER and FENCER attacked and suppressed the anti aircraft guns so that only 2 Barracudas were lost. TIRPITZ was out of action for three months. Further strikes in July and August were not successful as they did not achieve surprise and TIRPITZ was protected by a smoke screen so that pilots could not see the target. Only 2 hits were scored and one which penetrated the ship's armour did not explode. When TIRPITZ moved to Tromso she was within range of the RAF Lancasters which finally overturned her with 12,000 lb "Tallboy" bombs on the 12th November 1944.

For nine months in 1943 VICTORIOUS became the first British carrier to operate with the United States Navy in response to a request as they were short of carriers after the losses at Midway. 832 Squadron exchanged its Albacores for the new Avenger and after working up the ship joined with USS SARATOGA in providing air cover for landings on New Georgia in the Solomons. There was little air combat and the Avengers bombed shore positions. 832 also flew from SARATOGA on one occasion. SARATOGA paid a return visit to the Eastern Fleet in April 1944 when she joined with ILLUSTRIOUS to launch an attack on Sabang harbour at the northern end of Sumatra in the East Indies. In May a further strike was made on the oil refinery and harbour at Soerabaya in Java but the results were disappointing and SARATOGA returned to Pearl Harbor. ILLUSTRIOUS attacked the Andaman Islands in June and in July joined with the newly arrived VICTORIOUS to provide air cover for the fleet bombardment of Sabang. In August and September 1944 VICTORIOUS and INDOMITABLE sent their Barracudas to attack the cement works at Indaroeng and the harbour at Emmahaven both in Sumatra but again without good results. Attacks on the Nicobar Islands were made from 17th to 19th October.

VICTORIOUS with Albacores after landing.

There were now 4 armoured fleet carriers under the command of Admiral Vian of destroyer fame who had commanded the escort carriers at Salerno. The 4 were VICTORIOUS, INDOMITABLE, ILLUSTRIOUS and INDEFATIGABLE and all the Barracudas had been replaced with Avengers. Their first strikes at targets in Sumatra on 20th December were not successful and more success was achieved on 4th January 1945. The redesignated British Pacific Fleet under Admiral Bruce Fraser then sailed for Australia and the Pacific where it would take its place alongside the American Task Forces. This had been agreed between Churchill and Roosevelt despite opposition from Admiral King the American Navy's Chief of Operations. On the way strikes were made against oil refineries in Sumatra. The first on 24th January attacked Pladjoe, 43 Avengers carrying 172 x 500 lb bombs, with 12 rocket firing Fireflies and 50 fighters. As a result the refinery's output was halved for three months and the oil in storage was burnt. The fighters destroyed 14 aircraft in the air and 47 on the ground. On 29th January the refinery at Soengi Gerong near Palembang was stopped from producing for two months, 30 aircraft were shot down and 38 destroyed on the ground. 16 British aircraft were lost including an Avenger Commanding Officer and one other which hit balloon wires. This reduction by two thirds in the output of petrol was a major contribution to Japan's defeat.

The British Pacific Fleet (BPF) consisting of 4 armoured fleet carriers, 2 battleships, 6 cruisers and 11 destroyers joined the United States naval forces in the Pacific in March 1945 as Task Force 57 in Admiral Spruance's 5th Fleet. Their task was to neutralise the Sakishima Gunto group airfields to prevent their use by the Japanese whilst the Americans landed on Okinawa. The first two days of attacks began on 26th March followed by three days replenishing from the Fleet Train of over 60 ships. More strikes were made on 31st March and on 1st April INDEFATIGABLE was hit by its island by a Kamikaze but thanks to the armoured deck the ship was operational in an hour.

After more strikes from 5th to 7th April the Task Force moved to attack airfields and ports in Formosa from where the Kamikaze were thought to be coming. These were made on the 12th and 13th and the fleet headed for Leyte for a week's rest but this was delayed for more strikes on Sakishima as the American escort carrier group had been largely put out of action by Kamikaze attacks. More strikes were made with 50,000lbs of bombs on 16th, 17th and 18th April and they reached Leyte on 23rd after 32 days at sea. They were back striking the island airfields on 4th May and the battleships also bombarded with their 14inch guns. On the next day 20 Kamikaze attacked and most were shot down by the fighters but 2 hit the carriers, one on INDOMITABLE but went over the side into the sea, and one alongside FORMIDABLE's island. Again the ship was back in action within a short time, a large dent in the deck being filled with concrete. On the 9th there were more hits on FORMIDABLE and VICTORIOUS which destroyed aircraft but did not reduce the ships' operational capacity. Over the same period 7 American carriers were hit and made unfit for further action. The armoured decks had indeed proved their worth. FORMIDABLE unfortunately had a fire in the hangar on 18th which destroyed 30 aircraft and had to leave for repairs. After strikes on the islands the fleet returned to Leyte having spent 62 days at sea with only a break of 8 days at base. The squadrons had flown over 5000 sorties and dropped 1000 tons of bombs. They had destroyed 98 planes in combat and as many on the ground. 26 aircraft were lost in action and 134 in accidents, in the fire and by Kamikaze attacks. 85 aircrew and ships personnel were killed.

In July the BPF with its 4 carriers FORMIDABLE, VICTORIOUS, INDEFATIGABLE and IMPLACABLE joined the American TF 38 off Japan as TF 37. It had 255 aircraft. Between 17th July and 10th August the squadrons launched strikes against the Japanese mainland, on airfields, railway yards and shipping. On 24th July 6 Avengers, 2 Fireflies and 2 Corsairs seriously damaged an enemy escort carrier KAIYO which was later sunk by US aircraft. This was the only attack by the FAA on a carrier during the war. This was the typhoon season which considerably interfered with operations. Strikes continued against shipping in August by both Avengers and Corsairs armed with bombs. On one of these Corsairs from 1841 squadron on FORMIDABLE, led by Lieutenant Hampton Gray, DSC. RCNVR sank the escort sloop AMAKUSA but Gray was hit and on fire yet pressed home the attack and then crashed into the sea and was killed. He was awarded the Victoria Cross, one of only two awarded to the FAA during the war, the other going to Lieutenant Commander Eugene Esmonde RN who was killed with most of his crews in the abortive attack by 6 Swordfish in the Channel against the German SCHARNHORST and GNEISENAU in February 1942.

Three carriers sailed for Sydney on the 11th August leaving INDEFATIGABLE's Avengers to make the last strikes and its Seafires the last fighter combats of the war on the 15th.

The 11th Aircraft Carrier Squadron with 4 new light fleet carriers, VENERABLE, COLOSSUS, GLORY and VENGEANCE had arrived in Sydney with 72 Barracudas and 90 Corsairs too late to take part in the air war but were able to assist in retaking Hong Kong and other outposts. All available carriers were then used to repatriate released prisoners of war using their hangars as dormitories. The other task was to dispose of Lease Lend aircraft in the sea as the Navy did not want to pay for them and the Americans did not want them back.

Avenger with British Pacific Fleet markings flying over INDOMITABLE.

Barracuda after hitting the barrier. Note that the engine radiator has been broken off and is on the deck. The flight deck fire crews are quickly into action. Those wearing flame proof suits are connected to other firemen who can pull them out in an emergency. There are eight fire extinguishers of different types available. A very alert deck handling crew.

Flight of Martlet fighters with engines running just before take off. Wings being held down as aircraft was unstable in a wind due to the narrow undercarriage.

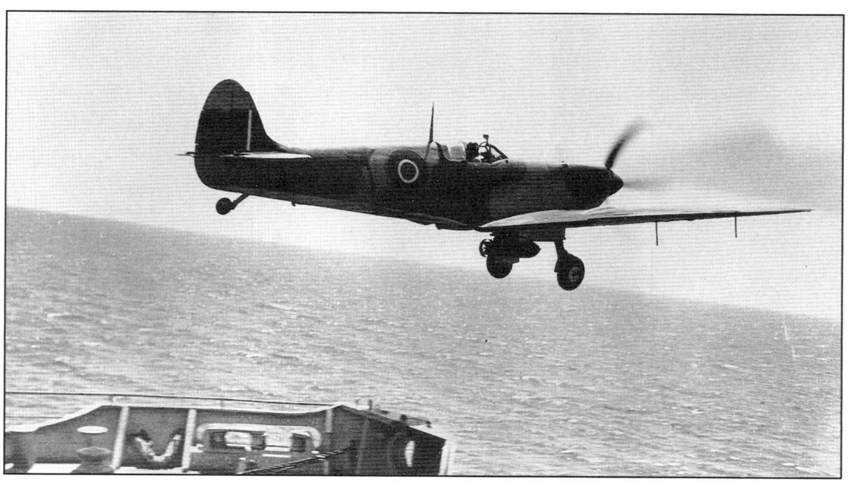

Seafire Mk.III of 899 Squadron taking off with a bomb from KHEDIVE. This was on operation Dragoon in August 1944.

The Next 35 Years.
Peace, Politics, Economics and Technology.

The years following the end of World War 2 were just as difficult as those after World War 1. During the next three decades most of the countries in the British Commonwealth became independent and in 1966 the Government decided that Britain should withdraw from East of Suez and restrict its military activities to opposing the threat from Russia in Europe. The Navy's planned new super carrier CVA-01 - 50,000 tons and a flight deck 900 feet long was cancelled and it was decided to phase out all aircraft carriers by 1980. The RAF was to take over the Navy's fixed wing aircraft and its role for defending Britain's interests overseas.

The FAA was fortunate that so many new carriers had started building during the war and it was these that were gradually brought into use during the post war years. No more conventional carriers were built. Successive governments had decided to spend less on the armed forces and more on other things especially social and welfare services. Nevertheless the Aircraft carrier has survived to provide what the RAF cannot, a highly mobile or protection force with commando support, using helicopters and vertical take off and landing (VTOL) Harrier aircraft.

Technology has also played a major part in shaping the post war FAA. The Light Fleet Carrier carried the latest propeller driven aircraft and the Firefly and Sea Fury were outstanding during the war in Korea in the early 1950s when Britain and the USA were the main allied forces fighting for the United Nations. These were soon superseded by the new jet powered aircraft and by the 1970s ARK ROYAL, the last conventional carrier, was operating Buccaneers and Phantoms together with Sea King helicopters. The introduction of faster and heavier jet aircraft had only been possible because of the invention by naval officers and civilians at the Research Establishments of the Angled Deck, the Mirror landing light and the Steam Catapult.

During the final stages of the war the jet engined De Havilland Vampire and Gloster Meteor fighters were starting into production. The Admiralty were considering how best to use this new type of aircraft and to obtain more information the third Vampire prototype was modified with extra flap area and fitted with an arrester hook. After trials at RAE(Royal Aeronautical Establishment) Farnborough on the 3rd December 1945 Lieutenant Commander E. Brown flew out to OCEAN. There he made the first landing on and also first take off from an aircraft carrier by a pure jet in the world. The Vampire had many good points for carrier work. It had a tricycle undercarriage, with its short nose the pilot had a good view of the ship's deck and the landing speed was low for a high speed aircraft. There were some problems as the engine response to throttle movement was slow and the fuel consumption was high at low altitude. After the first set of trials it was suggested that the aircraft would be unsuitable for normal carrier operation but further trials by Lieutenant Commanders J. Ievers and Pearson successfully evolved the technique for landing jets on carriers which is still used today. It was not until 1947 that 18 Sea Vampires were ordered for squadron jet training. Many hundreds of landings were made by these aircraft on carriers and the Vampire became the first jet aircraft to be launched by steam catapult and the first jet aircraft to land at night on a carrier. Two valuable years had been lost when the FAA could have gained more jet experience.

Vampire flown by Lieutenant Commander E. Brown making the first jet aircraft landing on OCEAN.

The progress of the jet aircraft was very rapid and thoughts of how to increase the performance still more occupied the minds of designers and users. To increase the rate of climb it was suggested that the weight could be reduced if the aircraft did not have an undercarriage. It was intended that the aircraft could be catapulted off from a trolley and on return to the carrier it could land on a flexible deck over inflatable rubber bags.

To test this possibility the Vampire was used. Trials were completed at RAE Farnborough and WARRIOR was fitted with a flexible deck. Both land and sea trials were completed and the system worked well. There was a problem of how the aircraft could be manoeuvred after landing and the time that this would take before the next aircraft could land. It was during one of the many meetings at the Ministry of Supply in August 1951 that Captain D.R.F Cambell who was chairing the meeting suggested that to clear the deck quickly the aircraft should be moved to a parking area on one side of the flight deck to be created by angling the flight deck by 10 degrees. A civilian technical officer Lewis Boddington was at the meeting. He was conducting the flexible deck programme as well as considering the layout of the flight deck of the ARK ROYAL. Due to the higher weights of the new aircraft there was also a problem with arrester wires and the strengths of barriers. In August 1951 Boddington produced a detailed drawing of an angled deck for ARK ROYAL.

At one of the regular exchange of ideas on naval aviation with the United States Navy(USN) the idea of the angled deck was mentioned. Later the Admiralty found out that the USN were planning to use an angled deck on the new carrier MIDWAY. TRIUMPH was marked with a landing path centre line set at 10 degrees to port. As the arrester wires were not repositioned only touch and go landings could be made. The trials were successful and the pilots enthusiastic but no action was taken by the Admiralty.

Sea Vampires F.20s about to be launched by steam catapult onTHESEUS

In May 1953 the USS ANTIETAM which had been quickly modified with an angled deck, visited the United Kingdom and invited the FAA to test the system. After these tests the Admiralty was persuaded and CENTAUR was the first to be equipped with 5 degrees angled flight deck and later ARK ROYAL. As it was now easy for the aircraft that had missed the arrester wires to go round and make another attempt, the number of wires could be reduced as well as the number of barriers. This provided a larger parking space for aircraft on deck as well as much needed space below the flight deck previously occupied by machinery.

With the increasing deck landing speed of the modern jet aircraft the information given by the Batsman was too slow for the pilot to apply corrections. It was fortunate that at this time increasing thought was being given on how to provide pilots with a visual indication of the approach and landing path. The RAF system of green, amber and red lights had been tried but the new system suggested was more complex and designed for carrier operation. The proposal was for a large mirror facing aft reflecting a light which was placed well in front of the mirror. This light would show the position of the aircraft in relation to a green bar on either side of the mirror. A light above the line meant too high and vice versa. So that the pilot could receive information while making a curved approach the mirror was curved. The whole system was stabilised by gyros and was installed on several British and American carriers. Later the system was further developed to the Deck Landing Projector Sight (DLPS). With this system the mirror was removed and there was a centre yellow light that moved up and down and a light on either side that showed varying amounts of red or white. Equal amount of red and white and the yellow light in the middle would show the aircraft on the correct approach path.

The other innovation to be included in all the modern carriers was the steam catapult. As the weight and the minimum flying speed of the modern aircraft increased it was becoming increasingly difficult for the catapult to provide the required acceleration. The use of steam as the accelerating force instead of hydraulic or air was proposed by a Royal Navy Engineer Officer Commander Mitchell and proved an immediate success. The length of the catapult was between 150 and 200 feet and could launch heavy aircraft without the 'G' forces on the aircraft and pilot being too great. As a later addition to the steam catapult it was arranged that the 'bridle', a six foot length of wire cable, should be caught at the end of the catapult and reused instead of being lost on every launch. This catcher can clearly be seen as a projection at the bow end of the catapult on ARK ROYAL.

Deck Landing Projector Sight. First type.

There have been continual developments in both ship and aircraft radar for the early warning of the approach of hostile aircraft, for fighter direction to protect the ships and for the control of the carrier's aircraft. There have been new defensive weapons and systems to protect ships and sonar systems to detect submarines. The aircraft's weapons have changed from cannon to rockets and missiles. The aircrew have ejection seats, personal distress radios and lights and special protective helmets.

HERMES in 1966 Sea Vixen FAW 2 of 892 Squadron and Buccaneers. One Sea Vixen on catapult with jet blast defector up. Spare strops on deck next to the retractable launch control cabin.

ARK ROYAL. Pilot's eye view when landing. The deck landing aid on the left hand edge of the flight deck is showing aircraft slightly high. Five arrester wires visible.

ARK ROYAL. A large number of Sea Hawks and Sea Venoms parked in the extra space created by the angled deck.

The Next 35 Years.
War-Worn Carriers.

Only ARGUS and FURIOUS of the pre war carriers survived and these were worn out and laid up until scrapped. There were over 40 escort carriers mostly on loan from America under "Lease Lend". These were all returned to the USA whilst the few British owned escort carriers were sold except for CAMPANIA which survived until the 1950s. There were six armoured carriers which had seen most of the fighting and 5 were in the Pacific. Their aircraft were disembarked and they were used as troop carriers to bring home the prisoners of war from Japan and the Far East and also servicemen coming home to return to their civilian jobs. ILLUSTRIOUS was already in the United Kingdom having a much needed refit which was then delayed as the war had ended.

These carriers were the pride of the FAA but needed large crews and were more expensive to operate than the economical Light Fleet Carriers which took over from them in the Far East. They all needed major refits not only to make good wear and tear and war damage but also to upgrade them for the heavier aircraft including jets which were coming into service. The government was more concerned with getting the country going again.

FORMIDABLE went into reserve in 1947 and was scrapped in 1953. INDEFATIGABLE and IMPLACABLE had less height in their hangars and were not suitable for modern aircraft. They were used as training ships with lecture rooms in the hangars between 1950 and 1954 and sold for scrap in 1955.

Both ILLUSTRIOUS and INDOMITABLE were modernised to operate the newer aircraft including longer and wider forward flight decks and served with the Home Fleet until 1954 and 1953 respectively before being scrapped in 1955. Only VICTORIOUS was fully modernised between 1951 and 1957 at a cost of £20m which was three times her original cost. The changes introduced all the modern developments such as a lengthened and strengthened angled flight deck with two steam catapults and a mirror landing aid. For the first time a British carrier was protected against nuclear fall out and had armament stowage for nuclear and guided weapons. New boilers were fitted and increased electrical generating capacity. From 1958 to 1968 she served in the Home, Mediterranean and Far East Fleets when she was laid up and scrapped in 1970 as part of the Government's Defence cuts.

The Aircraft Maintenance Carrier UNICORN was completed in 1943 and after supporting the Salerno landings provided support facilities to the carriers of the Eastern Fleet in Ceylon and the British Pacific Fleet. From 1946 to 1949 she was in reserve in Devonport and then returned to the Far East where she remained throughout the Korean War supporting the light fleet carriers and also ferrying troops when needed. UNICORN returned after 4 years in 1953 and again went into reserve until sold for scrap in 1959.

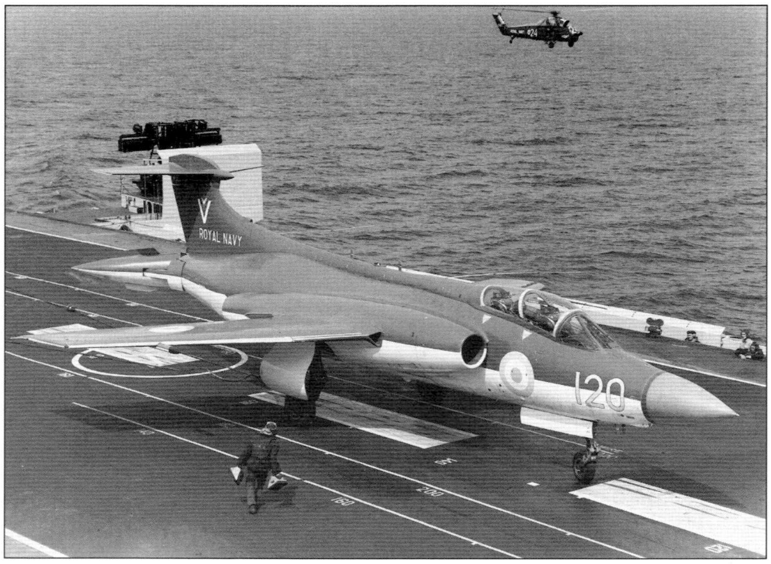

Buccaneer from 801 Squadron after landing on VICTORIOUS. Arrester wire has just been released and air brakes retracting. Deck landing projector sight behind aircraft and also the guard helicopter.

VICTORIOUS, with Scimitars on catapults. Also on deck Sea Vixens, a Gannet and helicopters. Ship is followed by ARK ROYAL and HERMES all with angled deck conversion.

The Next 35 Years.
COLOSSUS Class Carriers.

During the early part of the war the Admiralty were very concerned at the rate that the Navy carrier force was being depleted by losses in action. The armoured carriers were coming into service but the time between building and commissioning was too long. A way had to be found to provide the fleet with more ships designed from the start as carriers. In 1941 the first of the "COLOSSUS" light fleet carriers was designed. So that the ships could quickly enter service several important decisions were made. In spite of the success of the armoured carrier to withstand attack without sinking, the new light fleet carriers would not have armoured decks. To avoid the construction problems that a heavy defensive armament would cause it was decided to have only light automatic anti aircraft armament. The flight deck would be approximately 100 feet shorter than the "ILLUSTRIOUS" Class. As the naval shipyards were full of other naval construction the new "COLOSSUS" Class would be built to the standard Lloyds Register standards for merchant shipping and could therefore be built in normal yards. As speed of construction was most important the ships' propulsion system was that designed for destroyers which reduced the top speed to 23 knots, not as fast as the fleet carriers but this limitation was accepted to reduce construction time. The carrier would have a single hangar running the length of the ship served by two large lifts fore and aft. There would be a single catapult capable of accelerating aircraft weighing up to 15,000 lbs. This was later increased to 20,000 lbs when the ships were in service. Initially the number of aircraft was to be 24 but later the number increased to 40. Most of the carriers in operational service were already being fitted with early radar sets and this new class was designed from the outset to have long range and fighter direction radars. The defensive armament was to be a large number of either 20 or 40mm guns.

The programme was for 10 ships each weighing about 13,000 tons and construction started in 1942.

VENERABLE with Corsairs on flight deck.

Despite the efforts made to speed construction only four were to be fully operational by the end of the war. These were GLORY, COLOSSUS, VENERABLE and VENGEANCE and they were in Australia about to join the Pacific Fleet. Each carrier had 18 Barracudas and 21 Corsair fighters.

One other, OCEAN, was working up(completing the checking of the ship's performance and aircraft squadrons) in home waters. The squadrons embarked were equipped with Hellcat fighters and Firefly night fighters, the latter being a new role for carrier aircraft.

UNICORN entering Kobe harbour during the Korean War.

Following the success of UNICORN two of these light fleet carriers PERSEUS and PIONEER were completed as aircraft maintenance carriers. They were built to the same design as the other ships of the class but the flight deck was not used as such and contained large deck houses. The defensive armament was also located on the flight deck.

The three other ships of the same class were under construction THESEUS, TRIUMPH and WARRIOR and they were completed in 1946.

The original intention had been to have 16 of the "COLOSSUS" Class but the last six were to be able to operate heavier aircraft. These were renamed the "MAJESTIC" Class.

The flight deck had been strengthened for the heavier aircraft, larger lifts were fitted and improvements were made below decks. The construction of all six was started in 1943 and by the end of 1945 all had been launched and were fitting out. With the end of hostilities the navy had a surplus of carriers in service and under construction, so the six were laid up pending a decision on their future. Five of them were eventually sold to other navies and the sixth was scrapped in 1968 after a long stay in Portsmouth harbour.

Four of the original light fleet carriers also went to foreign navies. COLOSSUS went to France in 1946 as ARROMANCHES and took part in the Suez campaign in 1956. VENERABLE was taken over by the Dutch in 1948 and from 1958 had an angled deck and operated jet aircraft. In 1969 it was sold to Argentina and as 25th de MAYO took part in the invasion of the Falklands Islands in 1982. WARRIOR was operated by Canada from 1946 to 1948 and then by the Royal Navy before being sold to Argentina in 1958. VENGEANCE served with the Royal Australian Navy from 1952 to 1955 and was sold to Brazil in 1956.

OCEAN was used in 1945 for the first ever deck landing by a jet aircraft, the Vampire, and for other deck landing trials. WARRIOR was used for flexible deck landing trials. PERSEUS was used for steam catapult trials. Five light fleet carriers took part in the Korean War.

The Korean War lasted from 25th June 1950 when the Communist Forces of North Korea crossed the border with South Korea which was the 38th parallel of latitude, until 27th July 1953 when a peace agreement was signed. The Chinese supported the North and saved their forces from defeat in November 1950. A stalemate existed from June 1951 until July 1953. The United Nations sent forces to support the South as soon as it was attacked and this included British and American forces. Being so far from the United Nation (UN) bases naval forces and aircraft carriers in particular were an essential part of the force. The need for mobile air forces which only carriers could provide was once again proved in Korea. The British carriers employed in Korea were all light fleet carriers, TRIUMPH being the first to arrive from Hong Kong making the first naval strikes with the United States VALLEY FORGE on 3rd July 1950. She was later replaced by THESEUS and in 1951 by GLORY which alternated with OCEAN every six months until the end of the war in 1953. The Australian carrier SYDNEY which was one of the Majestic class of light fleet carriers, also took part in 1951 and 1952. The carriers were supported by the aircraft repair carrier UNICORN which ferried replacements from bases in Japan and Singapore in Malaya.

The carrier and squadron performances were outstanding and quite equal to their American allies. TRIUMPH carried Seafires and Fireflies. The later carriers had the latest fighter the Sea Fury and also the improved Fireflies. THESEUS completed 1463 deck landings without a single accident and during her six months in Korea her aircraft flew 5600 hours of operations and made 2361 deck landings. GLORY made 393 patrols at an average of 49 for every flying day, dropping 22 x 1000lb and 200 x 500lb bombs and 1500 rocket projectiles. This was also the first carrier to use Rocket Assisted Take Off (RATOG) and in March 1952 recorded the 5000th deck landing of the commission during her second tour in Korea. During her two tours GLORY's aircraft flew 4835 sorties for the loss of 27 aircraft and 9 crew, steamed 59730 miles, and used

PERSEUS. Note items on the deck of this maintenance carrier.

886330, rounds of 20mm ammunition, 13098 rocket projectiles, 3114 x 500lb and 126 x 1000lb bombs. OCEAN took over in May 1952 and on her first patrol flew a record 569 sorties in 7½ days with a record 123 sorties on the 17th May. The Royal Australian Navy's carrier SYDNEY spent 64 days in the operational area during the bad weather of December 1952. 12 Flying days were lost because of bad weather but 2366 sorties were flown in 43 flying days at an average of over 55 a day.

This was the last major war in which the main aircraft were powered by piston engines and also the first in which helicopters were used to rescue aircrew who came down in the sea or in enemy territory.

The Royal Navy's light fleet carriers continued in service until the late 1950s. OCEAN and THESEUS were both converted for helicopter use and were used to land the Royal Marine Commandos by helicopter at Suez in 1956. They then went into reserve until scrapped in 1962. GLORY was used for ferrying and as a helicopter base until 1958 and scrapped in 1961. TRIUMPH was in reserve from 1955 till 1965 when converted to a heavy escort maintenance ship, in which role it continued until 1972, being scrapped in 1981.

The Next 35 Years.

Centaur, Albion and Bulwark.

The "COLOSSUS" Class had been designed for rapid building and this had been achieved. However combat experiences with slower carriers had highlighted the requirement for higher speed and some increase in armour and armament protection. Consequently a new class of carrier was ordered. This was to be known as the "HERMES" Class and the first three ships were laid down in 1944. They were ALBION, ELEPHANT and CENTAUR. A fourth ship BULWARK was laid down in May 1945. Four more were to have been ordered but were cancelled with the ending of the war. The name of the ELEPHANT was changed to HERMES to perpetuate the name of the ship sunk by the Japanese. The order for three of these ships was almost cancelled with the end of hostilities but work was continued without too much urgency. The fourth HERMES was to remain on the slipway and was not launched until 1953.

The "HERMES" Class had more powerful machinery to give a speed of 27 knots. Some areas had increased armour protection. The hangar height was to be 17½ feet and the flight deck increased in length to 733 feet. The catapults were capable of launching aircraft up to 30,000lb all up weight(AUW). The aircraft complement was set at 50 aircraft. All three were launched in 1947/48 and were then laid up pending decisions concerning their future. One point in their favour was the height of the hangar as the older "ILLUSTRIOUS" Class had low hangar heights of 14 or 16 feet.

The decision to complete the three was taken in 1951 with a revised specification concerning changes in armament and the fitting of comprehensive radar equipment. The aircraft complement had been reduced to 40 and would include Sea Hawk jet fighters, aircraft for antisubmarine (A/S) and airborne early warning (AEW) duties. CENTAUR was the first to be commissioned and on completion of acceptance trials was immediately laid up for the flight deck width to be increased amidships so that an angled deck of 5½ degrees could be installed. On completion of the alterations CENTAUR was deployed in the Mediterranean and although initially equipped with Sea Fury fighters, she later changed these for the intended Sea Hawks.

CENTAUR spent some time in the Far East before returning home in September 1956 to start a two year refit. Steam catapults were installed with improved arrester gear and there were considerable changes to the radar installation. In 1961 the ship had further modifications to the catapults and arrester gear so that

CENTAUR with angled deck. Gannet landing with 2 Sea Hawks parked. Recovery helicopter on guard.

Large number of Wessex helicopters about to take off from a carrier.

Scimitars and Sea Vixens could be operated. The introduction of these larger first line aircraft besides the Gannet AEW and the Whirlwind helicopters reduced the aircraft complement to 20. Hangar space was a growing problem. The ship saw little operational service after 1965 and was scrapped in 1972.

The second of the three ships of the class, ALBION, was completed in May 1954. This time the angled deck was at 5¾ degrees, the largest so far. The ship was later modified to have mirror landing sight installed.

In 1960 ALBION entered the dockyard for a two year refit for conversion to a Commando Carrier. During the Suez campaign the use of helicopters to transport troops had proved very successful and with the changing role of the carrier it was decided that two carriers, ALBION and BULWARK, should be converted especially for this task. The modifications to the ships included removal of the hydraulic catapults, arrester wires and barriers and the mirror landing aid. The defensive armament and the radar were reduced. Davits for two landing craft were installed on each side of the flight deck aft of the island. This was for the transportation of heavy equipment or troops. BULWARK could carry 16 Whirlwind helicopters which could be converted on board to the A/S role if required. The accommodation of the ship was changed so that it could accommodate up to 733 men besides the ship's crew by using part of the hangar space. There was also space for the stores and equipment to keep the commando unit self supporting in the initial stages of an amphibious landing. BULWARK was later modified to accommodate 900 men and the larger Wessex helicopter. ALBION was converted in much the same manner except that she was modified from the start to operate the Wessex helicopter and accommodate 900 men.

BULWARK with helicopters and VICTORIOUS with large air defence radar.

Between 1962 and 1966 ALBION and BULWARK operated commando support helicopters in helping the Federation of Malay States and the British and Commonwealth forces against Indonesian insurgent forces. Help was also given in Borneo. ALBION was finally scrapped in 1973.

BULWARK continued in the Commando role until 1976 when she was withdrawn from service but this was not the end of her career.BULWARK was brought out of reserve in 1977 and underwent refit as an ASW carrier equipped with Sea King helicopters. The ship still acted in the normal role as a Commando carrier. Bulwark was finally scrapped in 1984.

Sea Furies on CENTAUR.

The Next 35 Years.

HERMES.

HERMES was the last of the HERMES class to be completed. Although launched in 1953 the plans for the carrier were continually being revised to take into account advances in ship and aircraft design. Eventually the carrier was completed in November 1959, a time lapse of 15 years between the laying of the keel and completion.

The major difference from her sister ships was the inclusion of a fully angled deck of 6½ degrees, a deck edge lift forward on the port side and a centre line lift aft. Two steam catapults were fitted, the port one being longer and starting in the angled deck. The arrester gear and the flight deck were stressed to accept the heavy aircraft now entering service, Sea Vixens and Scimitars. A mirror landing aid was fitted and the ship's radar was housed in a distinctive head lamp housing at the forward end of the island. The changes in ship design had not increased the number of aircraft carried, this remaining at 21. In the early 1960s there was a change in the ship's armament and some of the 40mm guns were removed and replaced by two quadruple Seacat missile launchers. In 1964 the ship was paid off for a long refit.

HERMES after angled deck conversion. Landing area, side lift, catapults and jet blast deflectors all outlined.

At the completion of this refit the flight deck area had been increased by widening on the port side to provide more aircraft parking and an extra area had been added on the starboard side of the island to allow for passage of vehicles. There were some radar changes and the mirror landing aid had been replaced by a Deck Landing Projector Sight. (DPLS). HERMES was recommissioned in 1966 and served until 1970, then being converted to a commando carrier to replace ALBION. The conversion followed the same pattern as the other commando carriers and was finished in 1973. Between 1977 and 1979 several trials were completed on HERMES with RAF Harriers from No.1. Squadron and also the prototype Sea Harrier. It was during the Falklands campaign that once again some Harriers from No.1. Squadron were to be embarked.

With the scrapping of ARK ROYAL in 1978 there was a need to fill the gap until the new INVINCIBLE class support carriers came into service. It was decided in 1980 to convert HERMES to carry a squadron of Sea Harriers and eight helicopters. The modifications involved the construction of a "Ski jump" ramp 150 feet long on the port side over the bow of the ship. This was inclined at an angle of 12½ degrees. The angled deck was retained. Other small changes were made and the refit was completed in June 1981.

HERMES played a vital part in the Falklands war when it was the command ship and remained in service until 1984, being sold to India in 1985.

HERMES after conversion to helicopter carrier. Still retains angled deck and side lift but arrester wires and catapults removed.

The Next 35 Years.

Fleet Carriers.

Four new fleet carriers had been ordered during the war. They were to have been AUDACIOUS, ARK ROYAL, AFRICA and EAGLE. The first, AUDACIOUS was laid down in 1942, ARK ROYAL in 1943 and the third, EAGLE, in 1944. The fourth was never started. Construction continued after the war but in 1946 building of EAGLE was stopped. To preserve the name AUDACIOUS was renamed EAGLE and was launched in 1946. It was to be 1950 before ARK ROYAL was launched. These were the last two fleet carriers to be built for the Royal Navy.

All the lessons learnt during the war were incorporated in the design of these two carriers. There was to be a double armoured hangar and the flight deck armour was increased. The height of the hangar was initially 14½ feet but this was later increased to 17½ feet to enable the larger American aircraft to be used. Protection against torpedoes was increased by stronger underwater construction. The weight of the carrier was 30,000 tons and it had a top speed of 31 knots. Due to all the extra room that had to be made for fuel and accommodation the weight increased to 45,000 tons. The overall length of the vessel was 803 feet and the flight deck width was 112 feet. There were two large lifts and two catapults capable of launching aircraft weighing up to 30,000 lb. Self defence armament was the same as the old fleet carriers consisting of 16 x 4.5 inch and 61 x 40mm guns.

Progress on building was slow and EAGLE was not completed until 1951. Improvements had been made during this time to the radar equipment. After acceptance trials EAGLE was used as a trials vessel for many of the new types of aircraft including Sea Venom, Gannet and Seahawk. The first squadron based on EAGLE was 800 with Attackers. This was the first time an operational squadron of jet aircraft had been based aboard a British carrier. EAGLE had been completed before the arrival of the angled deck and in the middle of 1954 the ship was withdrawn from service for a refit. The changes involved the fitting of an angled deck of 5½ degrees. The arrester wires and barriers were also repositioned. A new steam catapult was not installed at this time.

In 1959 the ship was paid off (withdrawn from service) and placed into dockyard hands for an extensive refit that was to last for five years. The major improvements were the rebuilding of the flight deck to an angle of 8½ degrees. Two steam catapults were installed and a deck on the starboard side of the island was added to allow passage of vehicles. The air defence of the ship was improved by the addition of 6 Seacat missile launchers. The new mirror landing aid was installed as well as much improved radar systems. To improve comfort the ship was fully air conditioned for the first time. As a result of the changes the ship could now operate up to 45 of the new generation of naval aircraft and the ship's weight had increased to just over 50,000 tons. In 1970 the ship was involved in trials with Harrier jets from Boscombe Down. The Phantom fleet fighter was now coming into service and even though trials had been carried out on EAGLE the decision was taken in 1972 to take her out of service because changes to operate Phantoms would be too expensive.

ARK ROYAL with the first stage of angled deck and the deck edge lift.

ARK ROYAL had started building only six months behind EAGLE but was not ready for launching until 1950 with an expected into service date of 1952. When almost complete the benefits of the angled deck and new catapults were obvious so the ship was converted. As installation of the steam catapults required the deck to be removed the opportunity was taken to angle the deck by 5½ degrees with all the alterations to the arrester wires and barriers. One important decision was to install a deck edge lift amidships for the first time on a British carrier. This served the upper hangar only. It was unpopular and was removed in a short refit in 1958 during which the mirror landing aid was installed. This was later to be changed to the Projector Landing Sight.

The Labour Government's Defence policy of 1966 required that the carrier force be phased out in 1974/75 and with the introduction of the Phantom the decision was made to refit ARK ROYAL instead of EAGLE to operate these aircraft.

The modifications were considerable, the flight deck was angled to 8½ degrees and two steam catapults fitted, both of which were capable of launching Phantoms in nil wind conditions.

ARK ROYAL Final conversion. Fully angled deck, steam catapults with bridle catchers, and Flying Control extended from island.

An innovation was the installation of bridle catchers to avoid them being lost after every launch. Radar modifications were also extensive. Apart from minor refits ARK ROYAL remained in service until 1978 when she was withdrawn .

Carriers were able to demonstrate their unique abilities in 1956 at Suez when the Egyptians under Colonel Nasser nationalised the Franco British Suez Canal Company. The French and British governments sent a combined naval force to prevent the destruction of the canal which was vital to their lines of communication with their interests in the Far East, India and Asia. Operation "Musketeer" began on 30th October when 3 British and 2 French carriers arrived off Port Said. Most of the aircraft involved were jets. For the first days the aircraft from the carriers and RAF aircraft based in Malta and Cyprus, attacked airfields and other ground targets in preparation for the landings on the 5th and 6th November. The airborne assault from Cyprus was made on the 5th and the main forces landed the next day, the Royal Marine Commando being taken in by helicopters from carriers THESEUS and OCEAN. The United Nations under pressure from the USA, called a cease fire the next day. There followed cease fire duties and ALBION remained for a month flying constant patrols. Both EAGLE and BULWARK completed over 600 sorties during the operation.

The FAA had once again proved it could provide close air support to land forces with immediate response and the maximum time at the required position as the carriers were so close.

After Suez it was decided to create a Strategic Reserve Force which could prevent war by intervention. In 1961 Kuwait which had a defence agreement with Britain, called for assistance when it faced possible attack by Iraq. Within a day BULWARK had arrived with 42 Royal Marine Commando which were landed by helicopter. VICTORIOUS was diverted from the Indian Ocean and agreement was reached between Iraq and Kuwait.

In 1965 Southern Rhodesia unilaterally declared independence and the United Kingdom Government imposed a blockade on its imports, particularly oil. This Beira Patrol was maintained by EAGLE and its aircraft, Gannets, Buccaneers, Scimitars and Sea Vixens, making day and night air searches. 770 ships were checked and 1000 operational sorties flown in a period of 46 days. In 1967 CENTAUR's helicopters landed the Royal Marines 45 Commando at Aden to keep the peace and subsequently ALBION and EAGLE covered the withdrawal of the British Forces.

By the early 1970s the Navy had withdrawn from east of Suez in accordance with government policy. The fleet carriers VICTORIOUS and EAGLE were paid off in 1968 and 1972 respectively leaving only ARK ROYAL until she paid off in 1979 when her aircraft were handed over to the RAF. The FAA was left with only BULWARK and HERMES and 3 Light Carriers being built.

ARK ROYAL. Pilots view. The latest type of nylon barrier up with spare cable on either side. This type of aircraft restraint caused less damage to the aircraft. Deck Landing Projector Sight on port and starboard side. Flying Control projecting from the island and aircraft parked beyond.

ARK ROYAL. Gannet testing engines. The water cooled jet blast barrier is raised to avoid air blast from the engines on aircraft parked behind. The search and rescue helicopter is standing by.

Two Scimitars on ARK ROYAL ready for catapult launch. Spare launch strops on deck. Aircraft nose raised off deck.

Sea Hawk with brake failure engaging the new type nylon barrier without damage.

EAGLE with slightly angled deck. Wyverns and Sea Hawks on port side in Suez markings. On the starboard side there are more Sea Hawks and Sea Venoms.

Vertical Take Off and Landing.
Policy and Politics.

Over the years since World War 2 the helicopter has evolved to become an important part of all air forces, not least the FAA. Traditionally carriers were always accompanied by a destroyer as guard ship to rescue any aircrew that might come down in the sea and amphibious Walrus and Sea Otter aircraft were used to rescue those further away. By 1950 Dragonfly helicopters began to be used for these duties and for communications. In late 1952 a squadron of Whirlwinds was formed and carried out troop support operations in Malaya. In 1956 Whirlwind and Sycamore helicopters carried assault forces from British carriers to land them at Suez and this resulted in the conversion of ALBION and BULWARK into commando carriers operating Whirlwind and Wessex helicopters. BULWARK later also used Sea Kings. By the 1960s Wessex and Sea Kings had been developed for anti submarine duties and were able to replace fixed wing aircraft. Unfortunately the Airborne Early Warning (AEW) role which detected the approach of enemy aircraft and missiles was passed to the RAF and the absence of shipborne aircraft with this facility in the Falklands operations contributed to the loss of ships. As a result the Sea King with AEW was developed and is now accepted as essential. Helicopters are now able to fill many of the FAA's duties but there is still a need for an aircraft for the defence of naval ships at sea, as well as for attacking ground and shipping targets in places too far from RAF bases. This role has been filled by the British invented and designed Harrier.

The prototype Hawker P1127 first flew in 1960 with the revolutionary ability to take off and land vertically. The first landing on a carrier took place in 1963 but it was not until 1980 that the first squadron was formed to embark on the new carrier INVINCIBLE, and a second joined HERMES in 1981. Even so both these carriers were due to be sold to Australia and India when Argentine invaded the Falklands in 1982. These two ships with their Harriers and helicopters were the key to the recapture of the islands. Harriers and helicopters have continued to demonstrate how they and the aircraft carriers are indispensable not only to Great Britain and its Navy but also to the United Nations which needs support in many parts of the world.

The use of aircraft carriers with Vertical Take Off aircraft has been adopted by several foreign navies.

HERMES modified for Harrier operation. Still equipped with the angled deck and side lift but no arrester wires or barriers. Take off path for the ski jump has a well defined centre line. Parking places for aircraft are marked with white circles.

Vertical Take Off and Landing.

Helicopter Carriers.

The success of the helicopter in various roles in the Navy lead to the development of specialised carriers that could support the commando carriers. The helicopter was limited in the weight of equipment that it could transport. In an amphibious operation it was necessary to have some way of supporting the Commandos with heavy armoured vehicles and equipment once they were ashore.

Two specialised ships were developed to cover this requirement. They were FEARLESS and INTREPID. The design was based on an original requirement for Dock Landing Ships during World War 2. At the time building commitments in Britain had prevented these being constructed but the design was passed to the Americans who constructed them and four were passed to the Royal Navy.

INTREPID. Wessex Mk.5. helicopter and vehicles on deck and two large landing craft in the rear dock.

The two new British ships were laid down in 1962. These were unusual as most of the after part was occupied by an internal dock which was divided into two sections by a centreline barrier. Each section could accommodate two landing craft. When the dock was required for use the ship was able to flood tanks in the stern so that the dock was lowered to sea level. At the forward end of each section of the dock there was a sloping ramp down which the heavy vehicles could be driven. It was possible to carry and load two fifty-ton tanks. The forward part of the ship contained two connected vehicle decks and there was a further ramp to the flight deck where vehicles and stores could also be stored. The flight deck was 180 feet long and 80 feet wide. There was no hangar but the carrier could accommodate up to five Wessex helicopters and two smaller ones if required. The area of the ship on either side of the rear dock could accommodate up to 370 men and the large superstructure contained accommodation for the ship's crew of 580. The conventional defensive armament consisted of two 40mm guns and there were also four Seacat missile systems.

FEARLESS was commissioned in November 1965 and INTREPID in 1967. The capacity of the ships was quite outstanding with a typical load of 8 landing craft, 16 tanks and 30 trucks of various sizes. If restricted space was accepted on the flight deck a further 20 three ton trucks could be carried.

Once both ships were in service they joined the commando carriers East of Suez and assisted in the withdrawal from Aden. As most of the British forces had now withdrawn from the Middle and Far East the ships were used in various exercises in the Mediterranean and Norway. The ships alternated being refitted and when the Falklands crisis started in April 1982 INTREPID was laid up. However within two weeks the ship was ready and joined FEARLESS. Each ship carried four Sea King helicopters and large quantities of stores. For the assault on the islands each ship carried 1500 men and remained off shore providing support for the ground troops. Their flight decks were used by representatives of all the helicopters taking part in the battle including the RAF Chinook. They even had a visit from two Harriers that had run short of fuel when their Forward Operating Base was out of action.

INTREPID at anchor. Four large landing craft out of rear dock and moored along side. Small landing craft swung out amidships. A Sea King and Scout helicopter on deck.

During the 1960s there was a need for fast ships to operate helicopters with the fleet to supplement the carriers. It was decided to use the cruisers BLAKE, TIGER and LION. The first two were converted but not LION and they came into use in 1968 and 1972 respectively. The guns aft were removed and a hangar and helicopter landing pad were built to take 4 Wessex or Sea King ASW helicopters. When ARK ROYAL was laid up these were the only ships able to fulfil the ASW role and remained in use until the late 1970s when BULWARK and HERMES were recommissioned for ASW duties.

There was also a need for a ship on which operational training could be carried out at sea. For this purpose LOFOTEN, a tank landing ship from World War 2, was converted with the forward deck made suitable for landing helicopters. It remained in use from 1964 to 1967 when it was replaced by the Royal Fleet Auxiliary ENGADINE which was specifically designed for the purpose. This in turn has been replaced in the 1990s by the new aviation training ship RFA ARGUS which can accommodate 12 Sea Harriers and 6 Sea Kings.

Orders have been placed for the next Landing Platform Helicopter (LPH) whose primary role will be the deployment of Royal Marine Commandos and helicopters and to provide airlift support to amphibious operations. It will be named OCEAN, be 20,000 tons and will be ready in 1998.

Wessex HAS helicopters of 845 Squadron transporting Gurkha troops in Borneo.

BLAKE with Wessex HAS Mk.3. helicopters flying over. The forward turret with high angle guns has been retained.

ENGADINE. Many years since the first ship bearing the name, the latest one still has a hangar aft but the landing area is greater. Wessex and Lynx helicopters flying past.

Vertical Take Off and Landing.

Harrier Carriers.

After the Government's decision in 1966 to phase out the carrier force, the Royal Navy needed ships to carry helicopters and provide command vessels to control anti-submarine forces. This requirement was temporarily met by the helicopter cruisers BLAKE and TIGER which carried 4 Wessex or Sea Kings. The new ships were designed to carry nine helicopters. As the Government wanted no more carriers they were called "Through deck command cruisers" and initially had a central superstructure but this was moved to the side as the design developed. The artist's impressions were taken from the side which gave the appearance of a cruiser. The first ship ordered in 1973 was given the name of a former battleship INVINCIBLE which became the name of the class but the other two were named after former carriers, ILLUSTRIOUS ordered in 1976 and ARK ROYAL ordered in 1978.

Whilst the ships were building the Navy was authorised to order the new Sea Harriers. The new ships were ideal for operating Sea Harriers but there was a problem in getting a fully laden aircraft airborne without using a catapult whose installation would be expensive and make the ship top heavy. Once again a naval engineer, Commander Doug. Taylor, produced the solution, a specially designed ramp "the Ski Jump". This was fitted at the forward end of the flight deck and enabled Harriers to fly off fully laden and without any other assistance. These were fitted to all three new carriers and also to HERMES which was refitted and modernised between 1980 and 1981 as a Harrier Carrier complete with the latest command, control and communication equipment.

The new ships were classified as carriers on completion and were 19,500 tons with a flight deck 600 feet long and a 480 feet long hangar below served by two lifts of a new design which saved both weight and cost and it was easier to move aircraft as there were no surrounding columns. The first two ships INVINCIBLE and ILLUSTRIOUS were altered to provide Ski Jumps of 7 degrees whilst ARK ROYAL had one of 12½ degrees as did HERMES. Each ship carried 5 Sea Harriers and 9 Sea King helicopters with a Sea Dart missile system for defence against air attack. There were the latest radar, command and communication systems. Four Rolls Royce Marine Olympus gas turbines provided the ship's propulsion giving 112,000 shp and a speed of 28 knots but they could cruise on one engine. A spare engine could be carried and changed at sea. In 1983 INVINCIBLE spent 166 days at sea which is a world record for continuous carrier operations.

INVINCIBLE was commissioned in 1980 and proved very successful but politics and economies again caused consternation in the Royal Navy when the Government decided that the ship would be sold to Australia in 1983 leaving only HERMES which would also be sold as soon as ILLUSTRIOUS and ARK ROYAL were ready. Events in the Falkland Islands off Argentina in South America changed such ideas. The Royal Navy and the FAA were faced with their hardest challenge of sending a task force to regain possession of the islands which were occupied by Argentina in April 1982. It was probably as well that Sir Henry Leach was the First Sea Lord and that the Chief of the Defence Staff was an Admiral too, Lord Lewin. Only the Navy and the Prime Minister believed that it could be done and it had to be done before winter fell on the Falklands in July.

The key to the task force was the two carriers HERMES and INVINCIBLE with Admiral Woodward using HERMES as his centre of operations for which the command, control and communications equipment so recently fitted was essential. All available Sea Harriers together with Sea King helicopters were embarked on the carriers. Some RAF Harriers later joined the task force. The assault ships FEARLESS and INTREPID were also in the task force along with other naval and merchant ships, many of which operated Wessex and other helicopters. The British carriers with their Harriers and Ski Jumps were always able to operate whereas the Argentine carrier was unable to fly off its aircraft on the day planned because there was no wind. Harriers were used for attacking ground targets and for fighter defence. The Sea Kings maintained anti submarine patrols around the Fleet, transported men and equipment, and supported the assault landing forces.

The one thing lacking was Airborne Early Warning (AEW) radar against enemy aircraft attack using bombs and Exocet missiles which resulted in the loss of several ships. An AEW fitted Sea King was quickly produced but was not available until the war was over and the Falkland Islands retaken. It was fortunate that neither carrier was damaged or sunk as without them the operation could not have been carried out.

With the subsequent sale of HERMES to India the 3 INVINCIBLE class carriers remain with one undergoing refit and modernisation whilst the other two are in commission. They are part of Britain's NATO force and are also used to support United Nations Forces.

Harrier just leaving the end of the ski jump on ARK ROYAL.
The increased angle of the ski jump is clearly seen.

INVINCIBLE followed by ILLUSTRIOUS.

INVINCIBLE and ILLUSTRIOUS. Both with Harriers and helicopters on deck.

ARK ROYAL with Sea King AEW helicopter and a Harrier.

British Carrier Index

Ship	Laid Down	Launch Date	Commissioned	Tons	Index Page
Ark Royal/Pegasus	7.11.13	5.9.13	10.12.14	7080	7. 8. 10. 11. 30.
Engadine		1.4.11	11.8.14	1881	8. 9.
Riviera		23.9.11	11.8.14	2500	8.
Empress		13.4.07	25.8.14	2540	8.
Ben-my-Chree		23.3.09	2.1.15	3888	11. 12. 18.
Vindex		7.3.05	26.3.15	2950	12.13.
Campania		8.9.1892	17.4.15	18000	8. 9. 13.
Manxman		15.6.04	17.4.16	2048	13.
Nairana		21.6.15	25.8.17	3070	13.
Pegasus		9.6.17	14.8.17	3300	13.
Argus		2.12.17	16.9.18	14550	14. 16. 19. 21. 22. 25. 29. 38. 44.
Hermes	15.1.18	11.9.19	18.2.24	10850	22. 23. 25. 28. 29. 37.
Eagle	20.2.13	8.6.18	20.2.24	22600	19. 22. 23. 25. 28. 29. 35. 36. 37.
Furious	8.6.15	15.8.16	26.6.17	27000	14. 16. 19. 22. 23.25. 28. 29. 36. 37. 38. 44.
Courageous	28.3.15	5.2.16	-.-.28	22500	22. 23. 25. 26. 28.
Glorious	1.5.15	20.4.16	-.-.27	22500	22. 23. 25. 26. 27. 28. 29.
Ark Royal	16.1.35	13.4.37	16.11.38	22000	26. 27. 28. 29. 34. 36.
Illustrious	27.4.37	5.9.39	25.5.40	23200	26. 34. 35. 36. 37. 38. 44. 45. 47.
Victorious	4.5.37	14.9.39	15.5.41	23200	26. 35. 36. 37. 38. 39. 44. 51.
Formidable	17.6.37	17.8.39	24.11.40	23200	26. 35. 37. 38. 39. 44.
Indomitable	10.11.37	26.3.40	10.10.41	24680	26. 35. 36. 37. 38. 39. 44.
Implacable	21.3.39	10.12.41	28.8.44	27000	26. 34. 36. 38. 39. 44.
Indefatigable	3.11.39	8.12.42	3.5.44	27700	26. 36. 38. 39. 44.
Unicorn	29.6.39	20.11.41	12.3.43	16350	26. 31. 44. 45. 46.
Audacity		29.3.39	-.6.41	5537	31.
Activity	1.2.40	30.5.42	14.10.42	12450	
Pretoria Castle		12.10.38	9.4.43	19650	31.
Nairana	6.11.41	20.5.43	12.12.43	14050	
Vindex	1.7.42	4.5.43	3.12.43	13455	
Campania	12.8.41	17.6.43	7.3.44	12450	44.
Colossus	1.6.42	30.9.43	1.12.44	13190	39. 45. 46. 47.
Glory	27.8.42	27.11.43	22.4.45	13190	39. 45. 46.
Ocean	8.11.42.	8.7.44	30.6.45	13190	41. 45. 46.
Thesus	6.1.43	6.7.44	9.1.46	13190	45. 46. 51.
Triumph	27.1.43	2.10.44	9.4.46	13190	42. 45. 46.
Venerable	3.12.42	30.12.43	17.1.45	13190	39. 45. 46.
Vengeance	16.11.42	23.2.44	16.1.45	13190	39. 45. 46.
Warrior	12.12.42	20.5.44	24.1.46	13190	41. 45. 46.
Perseus	1.6.42	26.3.44	19.10.45	12265	45. 46.
Pioneer	1.12.42	20.5.44	8.2.45	12265	45.
Eagle	24.10.42	19.3.46	1.10.51	43000	50. 51.
Ark Royal	3.5.43	3.5.50	25.2.55	43060	41. 42. 49. 50. 51.
Hermes	21.6.44	16.12.53	18.11.59	23000	47. 49. 51. 53. 55. 56.
Albion	23.3.44	6.5.47	26.5.54	20260	47. 48. 51. 53.
Bulwark	10.5.45	22.6.48	4.11.54	20260	47. 48. 51. 53. 55.
Centaur	30.5.45	22.4.47	1.9.53	18300	42. 47. 51.
Invincible	20.7.73	3.5.77	11.7.80	16000	49. 53. 56.
Illustrious	7.10.76	1.12.78	20.6.82	16000	56.
Ark Royal	14.12.48	2.6.81	1.11.85	16000	55. 56.
Fearless	25.7.62	19.12.63	25.11.65	11060	54. 56.
Intrepid	19.12.62	25.6.64	11.3.67	11060	54. 56.
Blake	17.8.42	20.12.45	8.3.61	9500	55. 56.
Tiger	1.10.41	25.10.45	18.3.59	9500	55. 56.
Lofoten	30.5.44	25.1.45	24.10.45	2140	55.
Engadine	9.8.65	15.9.66	15.12.67	8000	55.
Reliant	1977		1983	23000	
Argus	1981		1986	25000	55.
Ocean				20000	55.

American built Escort Carriers.
Archer. Avenger. Biter. Dasher. Tracker. Battler. Attacker. Hunter. Chaser. Fencer. Stalker. Pursuer. Striker. Searcher. Ravenger. Slinger. Atheling. Khedive. Ameer. Begum. Trumpeter. Empress. Emperor. Speaker. Nabob. Premier. Shah. Patroller. Rajah. Ranee. Trouncer. Thane. Queen. Ruler. Arbiter. Smiter. Puncher. Reaper.

CAM SHIPS
Michael.E, Primrose Hill, Empire Spring, Empire Tide, Empire Dell, Helencrest, Empire Rainbow, Empire Ray, Empire Faith, Empire Burton, Kafirstan, Novelist, Empire Stanley, Empire Shackelton, Empire Moon, Empire Wave, Empire Hudson, Empire Lawrence, Empire Eve, Empire Sun, Empire Heath, Empire Flame, Empire Clive, Empire Rowan, Eastern City, Empire Spray, Daghestan, Empire Foam, Empire Ocean, Empire Darwin, Empire Franklin, Empire Gale, Empire Morn.

MAC SHIPS
Empire MacAlpine, Rapana, Empire MacAndrew, Amastra, Empire MacRae, Ancyclus, Acavus, Empire Mackay, Empire MacColl, Empire MacMahon, Empire MacCabe, Empire MacCalum, Alexia, Empire MacKendrick, Miralda, Adula, Gadila, Empire MacDermott, Macoma.

AIRCRAFT

Avro	
Bison	27.
Lancaster.	38.
Type D.	4.
Blackburn.	
Skua.	27. 28. 29. 35. 36.
Buccaneer.	41. 51.
Blackburn.	
Dart.	27.
Borel.	6.
Bristol Scout.	13.
Caudron.	6.
Catalina.	36.
Chinnook.	54.
Curtiss Float.	3. 12.
De Havilland .	
Vampire.	41. 46.
Sea Vixen.	48. 49. 51.
Sea Venom.	50.
Fairey.	
Albacore.	35. 36. 37. 38.
Barracuda.	38. 39. 45.
Firefly.	36. 38. 39. 44. 45. 46. 41.
Flycatcher.	23. 25. 27.
IIIF	23. 27.
Fulmar.	30. 35. 36. 37.
Gannet.	48. 50. 51.
Sea Fox.	28.
Sea Plane.	9.
Swordfish	20. 27. 29. 31. 35. 36. 37. 39.
Focke Wolfe Condor	30.
Gloster.	
Gladiator.	27. 29.
Meteor.	41.
Grumman.	
Avenger.	31. 33. 38. 39.
Hellcat	33. 37. 38. 45.
Martlet	31. 36. 37.
Wildcat	31. 33. 38.
Hawker.	
Harrier.	41. 49. 50. 53. 54. 55. 56.
Hurricane.	29. 30. 31. 35. 36.
Nimrod.	27.
Osprey.	27.
Sea Fury.	41. 46. 47.
Sea Hawk.	47. 50.
Heinkel.	28.
Japanese.	
Kamikaze.	39.
Junkers.	
Ju.87.	35.
Ju.88.	38.
Maryland.	35.
Me. 109.	29. 36.
Phantom.	41. 50.
Short.	
S.38.	4.
Seaplane.	4. 12.
S.64.	6.
184.	8. 9. 11. 14.
Sunderland.	30. 35.
Sopwith.	
Camel.	13. 16.
Cuckoo.	16. 21.
Pup.	13. 14.
Seaplane.	9.
Supermarine.	
Attacker.	50.
Scimitar.	48. 49. 51.
Seafire.	31. 33. 36. 37. 38. 39. 46.
Sea Otter.	53.
Spitfire.	29. 33. 36. 37.
Walrus.	35. 53.
Westland Helicopters.	
Dragonfly.	53.
Sea King.	41. 48. 53. 54. 55. 56. 57.
Sycamore.	53.
Wessex.	48. 53. 54. 55. 56.
Whirlwind.	48. 53.
Vought Sikorsky.	
Corsair.	38. 39. 45.

SHIPS

Argentine.	
25th De Mayo.	46.
Australian.	
Sydney.	46.
British.	
Acasta.	29.
Achilles.	28.
Ajax.	28.
Audacious.	50.
Africa.	4. 50
Barham.	35.
Centurian.	21.
Cornwall.	37.
CVA.01 Carrier.	41.
Dorsetshire.	37.
Escort Carriers.	31. 33. 38. 44.
Exeter.	28.
Galatea.	8.
Hibernia.	4.
Hermes.	6.
Hood.	35.
London.	4.
Mac Ships.	31.
Majestic.	45.
Norfolk.	35.
Ohio.	37.
Prince of Wales.	35. 36. 37.
Queen Elizabeth.	8.
Repulse.	37.
Royal Oak.	9.
Sheffield.	36.
Slinger.	12.
Springbank.	30.
Suffolk.	35.
Valiant.	35.
Warspite.	29. 35.
French.	
Arromanches.	46.
German.	
Bismarck.	27. 29. 35. 36.
Gneisenau.	28. 29. 39.
Graf Spey.	28.
Hipper.	28.
Koningsberg.	12. 27. 28.
Prince Eugen.	35.
Scharnhorst.	28. 29. 39.
U.Boats.	28. 29. 30. 31. 38.
Tirpitz.	37. 38.
Italian.	
Caio Duillo.	35.
Cavour.	35.
Fiume.	35.
Littorio.	35.
Pola.	35.
Zara.	38.
Vittorio Veneto.	35.
Japanese.	
Amakusa.	39.
Haguro.	33.
Kaiyo.	39.
United States.	
Antietam.	42.
Birmingham.	3.
Midway.	42.
Pennsylvania.	3.
Saratoga.	21. 38.
Valley Forge.	46.

ABBREVIATIONS

A.C.N.S.	Assistant Chief of Naval Staff.
A.E.W.	Airborne Early Warning.
A.S.	Anti Submarine.
A.S.D.I.C.	Allied Submarine Detection Investigation Committee.
A.U.W.	All Up Weight.
B.P.F.	British Pacific Fleet.
C.A.M.	Catapult Armed Merchantman.
D.L.P.S.	Deck Landing Projector Sight.
F.A.A.	Fleet Air Arm.
M.A.C.	Merchant Aircraft Carrier.
R.A.T.O.G.	Rocket Assisted Take Off.
R.F.A.	Royal Fleet Auxiliary.
R.F.C.	Royal Flying Corps.
R.N.A.S.	Royal Naval Air Service.
T.S.R.	Torpedo Strike Reconnaissance.
V.T.O.L.	Vertical Take Off and Landing.

GENERAL

Accelerator.	23.
Aden.	12. 51. 54.
Air Board.	18.
Airborne Early Warning.	47. 53. 56.
Air Committee.	6.
Aircraft Carrier Squadrons. 11 A.C & 21 A.C.	39. 33.
Air Force Bill.	18.
Air Ministry.	20. 25. 26.
Airships.	3. 8.
Algiers.	38.
Anderman Islands.	33. 38.
Angled Deck.	41. 47. 49. 50.
Anti Submarine.	47. 53.
Armoured Carriers.	20. 26.
Arrester Gear.	22. 23. 25. 42. 47. 48. 49. 50.
Auxiliary Fighter Carrier.	31.
Balfour Committee.	19.
Barrier.	25. 42. 48. 50.
Batsman.	25. 42.
Battle Squadron.	33.
Beatty.	8. 18. 19.
Beira Patrol.	51.
Bell-Davies.	20.
Boddington.	41.
Bonar Law.	19.
Borneo.	48.
Bridle Catcher.	51.
British Pacific Fleet.	18. 38. 39. 45.
Brown.	41.
Burma.	33.
Cambell.	41.
CAM Ships.	31.
Carrier Proposals.	26.
Carrier Task Force.	8. 21.
Catapults.	23. 30. 31. 41. 42. 47. 48. 49. 50.
Chatfield.	19.
Churchill.	7. 18. 19.
Coastal Command.	19.
Colombo.	37.
Commando Carriers.	48. 49. 53. 54.
Convoys.	29. 30. 31. 37.
Coral Sea.	37.
Crete.	35.
Colley.	13.
Curzon.	18.
Cuxhaven.	8.
Dacre.	11.
Danby Committee.	19.
Dardanelles.	10.
Deck Edge Lift.	49. 50.
Defence Cuts.	44. 50.
Destroyer Flotilla.	33.
Dive Bombing.	21.
Dual Control.	19.
Dunning.	14.
Eastchurch.	3.
Eastern Fleet.	37.
East Indies/Egypt Seaplane Sqn.	11.
East Indies Fleet.	33.
Edmonds	11.
Esmonde.	35. 39.
FAA Museum.	9.
Falklands.	46. 49. 53. 54. 56.
Fisher.	3.
Fleet Train.	39.
Folding Wings.	6.
Force H.	29. 36.
Formosa.	39.
France-Landings.	33.
Fraser.	38.
Freeman.	13.
Geddes Committee.	18.
Geneva Disarmament Conference.	25. 26.
Goddard.	35.
Gray.	39.
Haldane.	19.
Hangar construction.	23. 26.
Hangar height.	47. 50.
Hankey.	19.
Heath.	16.
Henderson.	20. 26.
Holland.	21.
Holmes.	14.
Hong Kong.	39.
Ievers.	41.
Inskip Award.	19.
Iraq.	51.
Japan.	39.
Japanese Navy.	21.
Jellicoe.	14.
Jutland.	8.
Kaa Fjord.	38.

Kephalo Bay.	11.
Keynes.	19.
Kirkenes.	36.
Korea.	44. 46.
Kuwait.	51.
Leach.	56.
Lewin .Lieutenant.	28.
Lewin. Lord.	56.
Leyte.	39.
Lighters.	13.
Longmore.	4. 18.
Madagascar.	37.
Malaya.	33. 37. 48. 53.
Malone	8.
Malta.	29. 36. 37. 38.
Matapan.	35.
Mediterranean.	36.
Midway.	37.
Mirror Landing Light.	41. 42. 48. 49. 50.
Nagumo.	37.
Narvik.	29.
N.A.T.O.	56.
New Georgia.	38.
Nicobar Islands.	33. 38.
North Africa.	36. 38.
Norway.	38.
Norwegian Campaign.	28. 29.
Okinawa.	39.
Oran.	38.
Pathfinders.	35.
Pearl Harbour.	37.
Pearson.	41.
Peel.	19.
Petsamo.	36.
Radar.	35. 42. 45. 47. 48. 49. 50. 51. 56.
Radio.	4. 6. 20.
Rangoon.	33.
Ramsey.	20.
Rankin Darts.	13.
Rawlings.	20.
Reeves.	21.
Requirements in War.	21.
Rocket assisted take off.	31. 46.
Rotherham.	35.
Royal Aircraft Establishment.	31. 41.
Royal Air Force.	18. 19. 21. 25. 27. 35. 36. 37. 41. 49. 51. 53. 54.
Royal Flying Corps/R.A.N.S	4. 6. 18.
Rutland.	8.
Sakishima Gunto.	39.
Salerno.	31. 38.
Salisbury.	19.
Samson.	4. 11. 18.
Schwann.	4. 9.
Short.	4.
Siam.	37.
Sicily.	38.
Sippe.	4.
Ski Jump.	49. 56.
Slattery.	31.
Smuts.	18.
Somerville.	37.
Southern Rhodesia.	51.
Suez.	46. 48. 51. 53.
Sueter.	3.
Tactics and Equipment Manual.	20.
Tallboy Bombs.	38.
Taranto.	21. 27. 35.
Task Force.	39.
Ten Year Programme.	25.
Ten Year Rule.	25. 27.
Tondern.	16.
Torpedo attack.	11.
Towler.	13.
Trade Protection.	20. 26.
Trenchard.	18.
Trenchard-Keyes Agreement.	19.
Trewin.	8.
Trincomalee.	29. 37.
Tromso.	38.
Trondheim.	29.
United Nations.	41. 46. 51. 53. 56.
U.S.Navy.	3. 20. 38. 39. 42.
Vian.	31. 38.
Victoria Cross.	39.
Washington Treaty.	25.
Wedgwood Benn.	11.
Weir.	19.
Welsh.	9.
Western Desert.	36.
Williamson.	13.
Woodward.	56.
Zeppelins.	8. 13.